"The almost fairy-tale beauty of this powerful and hope-filled story could be anyone's catalyst to reach new heights and dream bigger!"

Nick Vujicic, speaker and author
of *Unstoppable*, *Life without Limits*,
and *Love without Limits*

"Jen Bricker's fearlessness, faith, and unflinching determination prove that anyone with passion and a sense of purpose can achieve their greatest dreams. I'm inspired by her—and you will be too!"

Eva Longoria, actress, producer, director, activist

"*Everything Is Possible* was a delight to read. It has stayed with me every day since I read it. Her tales of courage, adversity, inspiration, and humor make it well worth spending time with her on this incredible journey."

Pauley Perrette, actress, writer, singer

"Sometimes people are born under extraordinary circumstances and go on to live fairly ordinary lives. Sometimes they're born under ordinary circumstances and go on to live extraordinary lives. Jen is one of the precious few who was born under extraordinary circumstances and has gone on to live an extraordinary life. This is a special story about a very special woman. I'm blessed to call her my friend."

Joe Mantegna, actor

"Inspires in ways that *only* Jen Bricker can inspire. She's a true gift. This book outlines her magical life—from her amazing beginnings to her current impressive successes—with honesty, wit, charm, and ease. It's life-changing and heartwarming."

Tara Strong, actress

EVERYTHING
IS POSSIBLE

EVERYTHING IS POSSIBLE

Finding the Faith and Courage to Follow Your Dreams

JEN BRICKER

with Sheryl Berk

BakerBooks

a division of Baker Publishing Group
Grand Rapids, Michigan

Published by Baker Books
a division of Baker Publishing Group
P.O. Box 6287, Grand Rapids, MI 49516-6287
www.bakerbooks.com

Printed in the United States of America

The Library of Congress Cataloging-in-Publication Data
Names: Bricker, Jen, 1987– author.
Title: Everything is possible : finding the faith and courage to follow your dreams / Jen Bricker, with Sheryl Berk.
Description: Grand Rapids : Baker Books, 2016.
Identifiers: LCCN 2016012635 | ISBN 9780801019302 (cloth) | ISBN 9780801019395 (ITPE)
Subjects: LCSH: People with disabilities—Religious life. | Bricker, Jen, 1987– | Women gymnasts—United States—Biography. | Success—Religious aspects—Christianity.
Classification: LCC BV4910 .B75 2016 | DDC 277.3/083092 [B] —dc23
LC record available at https://lccn.loc.gov/20160126

16 17 18 19 20 21 22   7 6 5 4 3 2 1

This book is dedicated
to the glory of God.
May this book touch the lives
of millions around the world.

And to my parents,
Gerald and Sharon Bricker:
this wouldn't have been possible
without you guys!

Contents

Foreword

I first met Jen in September 2014 at an event in Beverly Hills. I introduced her to the audience and watched their reaction. They were instantly and completely blown away by her, just as I had been.

It was clear from that very first meeting that Jen and I had a connection. It isn't often I meet someone who shares so many of the same truths and goals: dream big; embrace what God has given you; bring light where there are shadows; spread hope, faith, love, and peace.

I love her relationship with God and how she inspires others to find Him. She does it not just through her words but through her actions. When she is face-to-face with adversity, she never lets it stand in the way of her joy and purpose. Her faith is unflappable. She is grateful not only for God's gifts but also for the opportunities to try and fail and grow. Jen and I have talked about how we both see our "disabilities" as advantages. God doesn't make mistakes; neither of us is a mistake. God knew exactly what He was doing when He created both of us.

A story like hers is so rare, and I'm proud of the fact that she is one of the few speakers I trust to take speaking invitations that I unfortunately cannot accept through Attitude is Altitude's speaking bureau. I'm proud of her for having the courage to truly put herself out there and share her story. But I also believe this is just the beginning. God has a lot more in store for Jen Bricker. Whether she's performing her aerial act or speaking before crowds of thousands, I can't wait to see her soar.

—Nick Vujicic

Acknowledgments

First and foremost, thank you, God. None of this, my life included, would have been possible without Him— my number one guiding force in all things!

My parents for being total rock stars and supporting every crazy thing I've ever wanted to try or do! My brothers—Greg, Bubba, and Brad—for loving on me since day one (and for not giving me a crazy name!) and teaching me how to "hang" with the boys and not to be afraid of getting dirty!

To my sisters Christina and Dominique, I cannot believe it's been ten years since we met. Time really does fly! I look forward to seeing what God has in store for the next ten years.

A *huge* thank-you to my entire community in Crawford County (teachers, coaches, and peers) for supporting me my entire life. I am beyond grateful to have the roots I have and a strong value of community from being raised by such a strong community!

Krine, you are the most amazing best friend anyone could ever ask for or dream of. I honestly can't imagine my life without you. I am *so* grateful God put us together!

Grant—you have always been on team J Bug from the literal second we met. Thanks for pushing me, loving me, and *always* believing in me!

I want to give a big thanks to everyone who took a chance on me when others were afraid. To all of you "angels" in my life who I come across in all my travels—thank you. You know who you are. You have let me stay in your homes. You have fed me, wined and dined me, and gone completely out of your way to show me love when you didn't have to. I will never forget who all of you are and what you have done for me. I only hope to return the favor to you one day—and more!

I need to give a big shout-out to my writer, Sheryl Berk. I honestly couldn't have done this without you—you are one amazing human being. I am extremely thankful to have spent so much time with you. Thank you for fiercely being on team Jen from day one!

Many thanks to Frank Weimann at Folio Literary for helping make this book happen.

To Joshua Schreff, my partner in crime, for always fighting for me.

Nick Vujicic for joining alongside me in such joyous and solid friendship.

Thank you to everyone at Reality LA. That church (all of you) has literally changed my life and is such an answer to prayer!

All my acrobats and aerialists, all of you who believed in me from day one. To Max, an amazing aerial choreographer, friend, and aerialist for helping me put acts together and have a place to stay and train!

Thank you to the *amazing* Jeremy Cowart, who made this beautiful cover an absolute slam dunk. You are fantastic, my friend!

Thank you to the entire team at Baker for being so excited and supportive of me! Brian, it has been an absolute joy working with you to make this book come to life! Amy, thank you for your enthusiasm along the way. Mark, you have been an absolute blessing. I seriously cannot imagine doing this book with any other company. I am beyond humbled and thankful for each and every one of you! You have made this process a totally beautiful one. Thanks for believing so strongly and passionately in this book and in me!

Introduction

Though she be but little, she is fierce!

—William Shakespeare,
A Midsummer Night's Dream

So this just happened: I flew into the IPC Athletics World Championships in Qatar, suspended from a giant hot-air balloon. Not the kind with the pretty wicker basket underneath, mind you. I was actually *attached* to the balloon with my fabric. I took one look at the setup and gasped. *This is amazing! I've never performed on a hot-air balloon before!* When the organizers asked me to come to Qatar and outlined their ideas for my performance, I had no clue how magical and epic it would be. The number I was a part of had been choreographed around my entrance—and they'd gone to a whole lot of trouble to blow up a ginormous balloon and have a three-man crew walk out holding it high above them. It was done with utmost precision. So, like anything else that scares me, I knew I had to go for it. In retrospect, it ranks as one of my all-time favorite "pinch me" moments—a perfect combination of cool and crazy, artistry and insanity. I mean, who *does* this? Me, apparently! The entire time I was floating up there, reveling in the cheers of the crowd below, a single thought kept repeating over and over in my mind: *God is so good!*

I have no doubt in my mind that I am blessed, though at first glance, maybe you'd think otherwise. It's kind of hard to miss: I don't have legs. But for the longest time, it never dawned on me that I was any different from anyone else. If there was something I wanted to do, then I did it. If I wanted to be a champion tumbler or an aerial artist, missing a couple of limbs was not going to hold me back. My approach was simple: no hesitation, no fear, no worrying "what if?" If an obstacle presented itself, I got creative and figured out how to get around it. It's an attitude that I feel people aren't taught, which is probably why I get asked for advice all the time. Life is an amazing journey if you're not afraid to live it.

That said, I have never felt like I have anything to prove. I am who I am, and I own it. People often ask me, "If you could have been born with legs, would you have wanted that?" Not a chance. God gave me this gift for a reason. And yes, I said *gift*. I don't see myself as "disabled" or "handicapped" or lacking in any way, shape, or form. I am grateful for my body every day. I wouldn't have been presented with such special opportunities to affect people in a positive way if I had been born with legs. That's how God works through me—through my "uniqueness."

Maybe from the outside looking in, it seems like I was dealt a bad hand. After all, my biological parents abandoned me the day I was born. But the way I see it, that was God protecting me. He had bigger plans. He knew He had to get me to the right place with the right people who could nurture my talents and gifts and teach me to embrace them. He knew what He was doing—He always does!

So yes, I am blessed. And my adoptive parents are my heroes because they taught me to see strength and beauty in places where others might not. They told me to keep going whenever a challenge presented itself. There were plenty of those and will continue to be many more. I took a Zumba class the other day and some lady asked me, "How do you do that?" Well, how do I *not*? How do I not kayak, skydive, roller-skate, play basketball—the list is endless. Ironically, I hate sitting still (and with no legs, it looks like I'm always sitting). I've been in constant motion from the moment I started crawling. It didn't matter that the first doctors my parents took me to told them I'd spend my life being carried around and propped up in a "bucket." The Brickers didn't see or want that life for their little girl. They never let anyone or anything hold me back.

Have I had moments where I've felt discouraged, insecure, frustrated, *crappy*? You betcha. It's called being human. I went through a long period of time as a kid when I had serious body issues. I didn't like what I saw in the mirror. I wanted to be tall and delicate with ballerina arms. Instead, I was short with body-builder biceps. I had to do a lot of soul-searching, and I arrived at the decision that God gave me this body for a reason. Then He gave me these talents and abilities to go with this body so I would catch people's attention, which is also my chance to educate, inform, and inspire.

That's part of what this book is about, but I also want to share with you all the intricacies of what makes me who

I am. Maybe you've read about me or even heard me speak. That's just scratching the surface. I am adventurous, artistic, intense, flawed, passionate, broken, silly, athletic, goofy, flirty, and playful. I am a sister, a daughter, a best friend, an auntie, an aerialist, a lover. I experience feelings of insecurity, doubt, fear, and weakness, and moments of absolute bliss, extreme adventure, intense passion, and heart-racing love. Sometimes I want to explode with joy, excitement, and happiness; other times I feel overwhelmed, underqualified, and lonely. I have never before shared so many aspects of who I am as a person. To be totally honest, I wasn't ready. I thought that strong people never reveal their weaknesses. But I know now that the opposite is true: it takes a lot of guts to be vulnerable and to put your whole true self out there. I'm not the least bit scared of twirling thirty feet in the air from a piece of fabric, but opening myself up . . . pretty terrifying.

But like every other challenge in my life, I knew I had to do it. I think what finally made it a surmountable task was finding my motivation. I want everyone who reads this book to realize one simple, amazing truth: you *are* significant. We all have special gifts and talents that make us not only unique but also great. Everyone has the power to change someone's life. Everyone has a voice and a stage and the ability to impact the world in a positive way. This isn't just about turning lemons into lemonade or seeing the glass as half full. It's taking action. It's pushing yourself to do what you were meant to do (let's call that *purpose*)—not necessarily what you are doing right at this moment. It's seeing beyond what's in front of you and imagining the endless possibilities.

Everything is possible. That's my favorite Bible quote from Mark 9:23: "Everything is possible for the person who believes" (GW). See it, believe it, make it happen. Who ever would have thought it was that simple? Yet my life is proof. The funny thing is I'm only twenty-eight, and I'm just getting started! I consider this the first leg of my journey (pun intended!). The path is clear—and I can't wait to see where it takes me. So ask yourself: Where will your path take you if you decide to push yourself to do what you were meant to do? Where might you find yourself that you never dreamed possible? It doesn't have to be soaring through the air on a hot-air balloon . . . but then again, why not? Don't knock it till you've tried it! Be brave. Dream big. Have faith. And don't be scared to look down. The view is pretty spectacular.

—Jen

CHAPTER ONE

The Baby Born without Legs

The Lord does not look at the things people look at. People look at the outward appearance, but the Lord looks at the heart.

—1 Samuel 16:7

I came into this world with no name—literally, a "nobody." My Romanian birth parents essentially abandoned me, leaving me behind at the hospital. And yet, I don't hate them. As hard as that is for people to understand, I have no anger toward them. Instead, I'm thankful. Thankful that because of what they did, I wound up in a loving home with my parents, the Brickers, who supported me and taught me that my life—every life—has a purpose.

Sure, it was a strange way to start a life. In a tiny hospital room in Salem, Illinois, my biological mother, Camelia, delivered me by cesarean section. I was born with big dark brown eyes, a head of thick black hair, dark brows and lashes, and very tan skin. I was also born with my heart on the right side of my chest instead of the left (many nurses got a scare when they tried to find my heartbeat with a stethoscope!). I measured a whopping thirteen inches, one inch longer than a ruler. Ironically, the hospital closed shortly after I was born. My family teases that after I was born, no one could top me, so they had to close up shop!

Camelia never actually laid eyes on me. That's because my birth father, Dmitry, didn't allow it—not even for a split second. A relative says the doctor who delivered me (also Romanian) told him I would die. Maybe he thought it would be too painful. Maybe he was trying to spare her pain or grief or regret. Maybe he just hit the panic button or felt ill-equipped emotionally and financially to care for a child who had special needs. Maybe he thought he was doing me a favor?

I don't know, and I don't pretend to know what was going through his head at that time. All I know is that he took one look at this tiny infant with two appendages where her legs were supposed to be and decided she'd be better off with someone else.

So no, I'm not angry, as crazy as that sounds. I don't blame my birth parents or judge them or hold any grudges. How could I when they gave me the greatest gift of all—a family that needed me as much as I needed them? My parents were honest with me from the start about my adoption. They didn't want me to feel hurt or abandoned or to hate my birth parents. They told me, "Jennifer, you have to understand, your biological parents were from a different country with a different mind-set. You didn't walk in their shoes, and you don't know the real reason why they gave you up. Whatever it is, it doesn't matter. This was exactly how God planned for it to be. You were an answered prayer, a miracle, for us. They gave us a gift; they gave us you."

It took a while for my adoptive parents to find their little gift though. A social worker first placed me with a foster family—a kind, loving couple whom I called Nana and Papa (I was with them for three months, but we stayed in touch for several years until they passed away). They named me Holly Ann. Papa worked on the railroad and always wore overalls, so I fit neatly in his bib in front, like a little baby kangaroo in a pouch. We would watch *ALF* (a weird little "alien life form" puppet for those of you who were not around in the late '80s!) on TV, and I had a little ALF figurine I carried around everywhere with me. They made sure I was secure and content, and months after I became a Bricker, my parents still took me back to visit them. They were the first people who loved me, and they truly had the biggest hearts. They fostered kids who were "hard to place" and saw a lot of sad, unfortunate children over the years. I wasn't one of those, despite my obvious "health" issues. Given my "specialness," you'd have thought that placing me in a permanent home would have been tough. But it wasn't—more than three hundred couples wanted me. I think about that sometimes: I could have been three hundred other Jens. It's almost like a math probability equation: If Jen went with x and y, what would she equal? The way I was raised helped make me the person I am today. I am grateful, so grateful, that God had this plan.

Praying for a Miracle

At the time of my birth, Sharon and Gerald Bricker—my soon-to-be parents—were living in Hardinville, Illinois, a tiny town in the middle of nowhere on the eastern side of the state. They already had three boys: Greg, Brian (aka Bubba), and Brad, who were fourteen, twelve, and ten years old. Nonetheless, they desperately wanted a baby girl. My mother had to have a hysterectomy because she had cysts on her ovaries, and she knew she would never be able to give birth to any more children. So she asked God for a miracle. She kept her faith, believing all along, *There must be one little girl in the world who needs this family*. The woman seriously has the patience of a saint!

One day a friend who was adopting called her to say she'd heard about me. My mom knew at that moment her prayers had been answered. She told my dad, and he was as excited as she was. Then they both ran it by my brothers. My parents asked Greg, my oldest brother, "How will you feel about bringing your date to the house and introducing her to your sister who has no legs?" Greg didn't even have to think about it. He said, "If someone can't accept her, I wouldn't want to date her." They went through every scenario with my brothers to make sure they were okay with it. Then, when the whole family was on board, they put the plans in motion.

My mom said she was 100 percent honest. She told the social worker all the reasons why our family didn't need more children and all the reasons why, in her heart, she knew she *had* to have me. It took two and a half months before my parents could actually meet me. During that whole time of waiting, they never saw a single picture of me, which was on purpose. The adoption agency and social workers wanted to be sure how the prospective new parents would react after meeting me and how they'd handle changing and feeding me.

My mom says she was a nervous wreck the night before, tossing and turning in bed and worrying about how I'd take to them. All those worries melted away as soon as they walked in the door of my foster family's home. My face lit up in a huge grin. My mom says that at that moment, she knew it was meant to be. It felt like she'd found the missing piece to her soul, and the smile on my face said, *You're finally here.* It was an instant connection, and taking care of me came to my parents instinctually. While my foster parents had struggled to change my diapers (I was a slippery little thing!), my mom was a pro. "It's so easy!" she exclaimed. "There are no little legs in my way!"

From that day on, I was Jennifer Bricker. My brothers were allowed to name me, but there was a catch: they had to agree on a name. They argued over it for hours until one of them said, "Jennifer," and they all kind of nodded in agreement. My mom tells me I went through a bit of an adjustment period while getting to know my new family. For two weeks I refused to crack a smile. Then one day one of my brothers sneezed and I burst into hysterical laughter. So he kept sneezing over and over so they could get their first picture of me smiling! That was it; I was a jolly little baby from that day forward. My brothers each had their own thing that they would do with me. Greg liked to rest me on his chest when he was doing homework; Bubba would stick me in the front of his bib overalls and carry me around; and Brad always fed me my bottle. They were so excited to have a little sister—I was like a shiny new toy!

The social workers made an appointment at the Cardinal Clinic in St. Louis, Missouri, for my parents to take me for a comprehensive medical evaluation. The prognosis was bleak: the doctors wanted to make me a "bucket" to sit in. In their opinions, I would never be able to sit up, crawl around, or move from place to place at all without being carried. My mom sat in the doctors' office and cried her heart out. But my dad did not agree with their prognosis. "No," he insisted. "That's not what she's about. We don't accept that."

So they took me to a new set of doctors, this time at Shriners Hospitals for Children in St. Louis. "I want to know," my dad asked them. "Will she be able to sit up? What does her future look like?"

This time, the news was encouraging. The doctor smiled and said, "Mr. and Mrs. Bricker, this little girl is going to do things you never even imagined would be possible."

But yes, they *could* imagine it. And from then on, we all had the attitude of *Let's go for it*. Nothing would stand in my way. My parents never held the reins too tight, but they also didn't let me fly in the wind with no rules. What went for my brothers went for me. Just because I had no legs didn't mean I received special privileges or treatment. I was going to grow up a normal little girl, and my parents would never accept anything less. They didn't coddle me or speak to me in baby talk. I was a talker—and very vocal about what I wanted— from the moment I opened my mouth. It started with me pulling myself up in the crib. "Hold you, Mommy!" I would call, meaning, "Hold me!" Not only could I sit up, but also I could move—fast! Faster than my poor parents could keep up with me. My mom called me "mouse" because I would scoot about with lightning speed. I used to pull myself along with my little arms and leave a trail of pink Pampers shredded on the ground behind me. My brothers had me practically jumping off the couch from the moment I could crawl around. They put pillows down to break my fall, but they'd egg me on. I never could turn down a dare. I was fearless.

Before I was five, I needed two surgeries: one to remove a growth plate, a partial bone growing down from my hip, the other to remove the two appendages so I could better tolerate my prosthetics. My family nicknamed the appendages my "flippers." One had the cutest big toe and a little arch and a heel, and the other was a little more unformed. As a baby, I loved music and would use them to keep time with the beat. Because I was so young, I don't remember much about those times going into the hospital. But my parents tell me I was never afraid, never sad to spend time there. The nurses all loved me, and I assured them, "Don't worry, I fine!" I was a tough one.

— My VIPs —

In these boxes, you'll meet the most important people in my life as they share their memories of yours truly. I'm humbled and a little mortified, but mostly humbled.

My Mom: Sharon Bricker

When I told my father, Noble Waldrop, we were adopting a baby girl, he hesitated. Not because of the way she was born, but because he wasn't sure he could love her the same as his other grandkids. She wasn't his blood. Well, that changed in a heartbeat. I took her over to my parents' house, and he fell head over heels for her. They had a very tight, special bond, especially during his last days. Jennifer brought him joy and comfort. He would get depressed being on an oxygen tank, and my mom would call and ask that we bring her by. Whenever we did, he'd immediately perk up. I remember she would sing to him to lift his spirits—she was the best kind of medicine for whatever ailed him. I remember watching her and thinking how she had a natural ability to connect with people. Today, whenever she speaks in front of a crowd, it's as if she's talking personally to each and every person in that room. She has more friends than anyone I know, and it's because anyone who meets her instantly loves her. I think of her with my father and how I knew way back then that she had a God-given gift for inspiring people.

I Can Do That

As I got a little bigger, my personality really started to shine through. I was trouble with a capital T! Growing up with three older brothers certainly contributed to this. Greg taught me to rock out to Garth Brooks. He also took me on many of his dates, probably because I was such an up-front little squirt—I'd give him my honest opinion! All my brothers would brag to their friends about how strong I was, and as a result, few would ever take on the challenge of arm wrestling me. They didn't want to get whipped by a little girl. As an adult, I can see that growing up with brothers helped me understand guys a lot better. To be totally honest, they're easier to get along with than most girls—less drama. Most of the friends in my life now are guys, and almost all of my roommates have been as well. I guess I miss living in a house filled with men!

I also have a sister, Jodi, my dad's daughter from a previous relationship before he married my mom. She's about fifteen years older than I am. I didn't get to see her very much growing up because she lived a few states away. But she would always try and remember my birthday. She would also come to see us for Christmas, which was always awesome. As I've gotten older, I've been able to see her a bit more because of my travel, and I try to let her know whenever I'm in Colorado so we can meet up.

As a kid, anything physically challenging—a sport, a game, a tree to climb—had my name on it. My parents tell this funny story about how, when I was a baby, I loved water and they wanted me to swim. They put little pool floaties on my arms, and when they lowered me into the water and let go, my butt floated straight up and my head went underwater. It scared my parents to death! Clearly, regular floaties weren't going to work, so they got me a one-piece suit with a little inner tube attached to it. That managed to keep my booty underwater. But when I was about six, I decided I'd rather dive down deep than float up top. I jumped in, sans floaties, and my parents let me go. It turns out I was a natural swimmer! In fourth grade, my school held swimming classes at the local college, Lincoln Trail College, in Robinson, where I placed into advanced swimming. I loved holding my breath underwater, and one day while I was swimming at the city pool in Robinson, I decided to challenge myself: How long could I stay at the bottom and not bob up for air? Reggie, the lifeguard, thought I was drowning and dove in to rescue me. I remember he dove in, lifted me up, and then held me above the water.

"What are you doing?" I asked, laughing.

He was embarrassed, but I didn't mind one bit. I had a huge crush on Reggie, and anytime he wanted to "save" me, I was fine with it!

My parents trusted that I always knew what I could and couldn't handle. They let me leap into the pool—and leap into my life. They treated me like a person instead of a child, even at an early age. I think that's why I learned to talk and spell and read so quickly. Everyone in my family did, so it was expected of me as well. I loved Dr. Seuss books and could recite *Marvin K. Mooney Will You Please Go Now* and *Green Eggs and Ham* by heart. When my kindergarten teacher asked if I could read them to her, I declared, "Absolutely!" But really I had just committed them to memory from my family reading them to me over and over. I've kept this secret until now—my teacher thought I was a genius!

My parents also never worried about what people would think of me. Initially, my mom said this little prayer: "God, please let her face be pretty so people don't notice that she has no legs!" For the record, she says God came through on that as well—but she's a little biased! And I guess I hadn't learned humility yet. When people would stop and tell me, "Oh, aren't you so cute!" I'd answer back, "I know it!"

My mom would turn twenty shades of red.

"Jennifer!" she would tell me. "We don't say that! We say thank you."

So then I would reply, "Thank you. I know it!"

People simply forgot—literally—that I was missing my lower limbs. In fact, my mom's best friend since high school has a daughter three and a half months younger than I am, and she was always sending clothes that her child had outgrown. One day my mom received a box of these hand-me-downs and opened them up to find an entire pile of socks and shoes. She called her friend, laughing, and asked, "And what am I supposed to do with these?" Her friend was shocked and embarrassed; she'd completely forgotten I didn't need them. But that's how it always was. People in my small town were so comfortable with me that they quickly forgot I was different. And because they forgot, I did as well.

I got my first set of prosthetic legs when I was a toddler—sometime around two years old. At first I screamed and hated how they pinched and poked and weighed me down. They were so foreign, so heavy and bulky, and I was too little to understand why my parents were pinning them on. As I got older and became used to them, I loved them. I could wear fancy socks and shoes, and I wore them to kindergarten. One day I went to the bathroom and left them there by accident.

A classmate went in after me and returned to the classroom white as a ghost. "There are legs in the bathroom!" he cried to the teacher, who promptly took me aside and reminded me not to leave them lying around. As I got older, I became more active and didn't want to wear the prosthetics much at all. Eventually, I wore them solely for dress-up.

The first sport I participated in was softball, which I played in first through third grade. I had so much hair that the helmets barely fit my head because of my giant ponytail. My brothers and coaches taught me to hit to the third baseline to give myself more time to reach the bases. But we all soon realized I was lightning fast—all you really saw was a trail of dust in my wake. I remember one time I hit the ball right to the first baseman. No one thought I would make it to the base in time, but I kept running. I didn't take my eyes off that base, and as the first baseman was trying to pick up the ball, I dove and touched the bag. *Safe!* It was a great lesson and a reminder for me: I should never take my eyes off my goals or God's promises for my life. Even when something looks absolutely impossible—game over—in that very last second, things can change.

While softball was about being close to the ground, the trampoline was about soaring to the sky. I played this game called Popcorn, in which I challenged people to see who could bounce the highest (I always won). I decided I could play basketball too, and my forte was stealing the ball. It was definitely harder to make a basket because I was so low to the ground, but I just had to throw that much harder.

I also decided to try volleyball in sixth grade because Mr. Corn was the coach, and he was effortlessly cool. He taught art as well, and I've always been drawn to artists, although my own "artistic soul" hadn't quite emerged yet. Because he saw I needed to build my confidence on the volleyball court, he definitely did not take it easy on me. I was extremely self-conscious and nervous about serving. Since I was so low to the ground, it was difficult to serve from all the way in the back of the court. Time after time, my ball wound up in the net. So he taught me to stand sideways and hit the ball that way. Of course, I wasn't the star spiker of the team, but I was great as middle back. Right where the ball dropped low, guess who was already low and didn't have to fall to her knees? This girl.

I think everyone who knew me was just waiting to see what I would do next. I kept doing things I wasn't "supposed" to be able to do. My parents were the only ones not surprised by my physical shenanigans. When I wanted to try something new and said in frustration, "I can't do it!" they would scold me. "*Can't* is a bad word in our home, and you shouldn't use it, Jennifer," they would say. So I grew up embracing the idea that I could do anything if I set my mind to it, just like the train in one of my favorite stories, *The Little Engine That Could. I think I can, I think I can.* To this day, I love the lessons that story teaches: be courageous, persevere, believe. As we try new things, we discover how strong we are and realize the only limits are the ones we impose on ourselves.

One day I told my parents I wanted to go roller skating, never even considering that I might need feet to put on roller skates. When you live in the middle of nowhere, you have limited activities, so the roller rink was the place to be! I asked my parents to take me to the store to buy a pair of skates, which they did, without any hesitation. The sales clerk must have thought we had lost our minds! *What is this girl going to do with roller skates?* If I thought I could skate, then my parents believed not only that I could but also that I would. I put the skates on my hands and off I went. It took me a while to make it all the way around the rink—and even longer to learn how to skate backward. But I simply refused to quit trying. And when I did make it around, everyone applauded. I felt like such a star!

My favorite moment at the rink was when they called, "Limbo!" Because I was so small, I could limbo like nobody's business. How low could I go? They'd never seen anything like it!

Seeing through God's Eyes

I had the happiest, most normal childhood. I collected Beanie Babies, Polly Pockets, and fuzzy-haired troll dolls by the dozen. One day I was walking in town with one of my favorites—a troll with bright blue hair—and a lady on the street remarked, "What an ugly baby you have there!" I swear my mom wanted to smack her because she saw how upset her words had made me.

"Mama," I wailed, "she called my baby uggy!"

My mother took me aside and gently explained that every creature is beautiful in God's eyes. "Your baby isn't uggy," she told me. "That lady was just having a bad day."

And that's how I grew up—knowing I was beautiful and perfect in God's eyes. Our physical presence is only part of who we are as human beings. What's inside is just as important, and maybe more so. My parents took me into their home and their lives with the fullest of hearts and the biggest of faiths. They knew life wouldn't always be easy for me. They knew I would experience frustration and pain and people who saw me in the way that lady saw my troll doll. They also knew they couldn't always protect me. I had to learn to fend for myself. However, they believed God gave me to them for a reason, and they felt an enormous responsibility to prepare me as best they could to tackle whatever challenges came my way. *Can't* was never an option. Fear was never an option. I would rather fall flat on my face than regret not trying. And I'm blessed with parents who were courageous enough to let me try, let me fail, and let me find my way and my trust in God.

My parents were very open about where I came from and the fact that I was adopted. They never thought it should be a source of shame or embarrassment. Some kids are born to their parents. Others are chosen. My mom says that one day when I was little, I asked her, "Mommy, do you think my parents gave me up because I didn't have legs?" She thought long and hard before answering.

"Jennifer," she said softly, "Mommy's tummy was broken, and God found you a really nice lady with a nice tummy so she could hold you until I could get to you."

I never questioned it again. It made perfect sense to me, and honestly, it still does.

BELIEVE IT!

These are the things I've come to know and believe with all my heart and soul. Think about them. Consider how they might apply to your own life or situation, and use them wherever and whenever you see fit. I'm not going to "school" you or tell you what to do. That's just not who I am (although my brothers might disagree since they think I can be pretty bossy). But I will tell you this: all the knowledge in the world won't do you any good if you sit on it. When you learn something, you need to put it into play. Otherwise, it's like holding the basketball and never taking that jump shot!

Everything Happens for a Reason

Trust that every experience—good, bad, or ugly—shapes the person you are for the better. Every mistake or misfortune is an opportunity to grow and learn. It's a matter of seeing the bigger picture, the purpose you are working toward, and how each thing you go through is part of the journey. I was born without legs. I could choose to have a woe-is-me attitude, and I don't think anyone would hold that against me. But I don't . . . ever. Instead, I see my body as a huge advantage because it provides me with the opportunity to have an extremely unique perspective on life. It also allows God to work through me to inspire and motivate others.

Sure, my life is more difficult in some aspects. I'd be lying if I said otherwise. But it would be too easy to go down that negative road. Instead, I prefer to focus on all the positives that having no legs has brought to my life: the opportunities, the people, the chance for my voice to be heard. And when I do think of all those things, the good overwhelmingly overshadows the bad. Bottom line: if I hadn't been born without legs, I wouldn't have the life I have now. And I certainly wouldn't be writing this book!

CHAPTER TWO

A Bundle of Energy

I can do all things [which He has called me to do]
through Him who strengthens *and* empowers me [to
fulfill His purpose—I am self-sufficient in Christ's
sufficiency; I am ready for anything and equal to
anything through Him who infuses me with inner
strength and confident peace.]

—Philippians 4:13 AMP

We had two mules growing up, Sady and Sam. I rode horses and mules, despite having no legs to put into the stirrups. I just figured out a way to plant my butt in the saddle and balance my weight, sure and steady. One time I was riding Sam and something spooked him, so he turned sharply to the right and directly into a clothesline. I ducked down, and then he jolted and started running toward the road and off our property. I fell off to the side and was hanging on to the horn of the saddle with only one hand. He kept galloping away at full speed down the street, but I refused to let go. I remember glancing back at my parents and brothers chasing after us in a panic.

"Stop screaming!" I shouted at them. "Calm down!" I was cool as a cucumber.

They eventually got Sam to slow down and hop back on the grass. When he finally came to a stop, I was still hanging on, stubborn as a mule myself. I gave my family a scare, but I was just fine—not even a scratch. Sam and I kind of liked our little escape act!

I never ran out of steam as a child. Seriously, I was like the Energizer Bunny. Anyone given the task of getting me to slow down had a huge problem. Slow wasn't one of my speeds, and frankly, I didn't come with any brakes. My elementary school hired a lovely lady named Penny Carman to serve as my personal aide in kindergarten. I didn't need anyone's help, and I quickly informed Penny of this fact. No, I didn't need assistance getting on and off the school bus. No, I wasn't disabled. No, I didn't need to make a scene everywhere I went. I could get around on my own perfectly fine, thank you. I might have given her a little bit of 'tude for a five-year-old, but Penny understood. She knew I desperately wanted to look and feel like a "regular" kid. The wheelchair wouldn't cut it.

"Can't I just ride in a wagon?" I asked. "You can pull me in it!"

So she made a few calls and got a sturdy little red wagon donated specifically for my use. I thought I looked pretty cool rolling in, and even better, all the kids wanted a ride.

Recess was one of my favorite times of the school day because I craved being outside, playing in the rocks, swinging really high (too high) on the swings, and dangling from the monkey bars. I was always the last one standing on the merry-go-round, while all the other kids stumbled off, dizzy. By God's good graces, I rarely wound up with more than a bump, bruise, or scratch. I would try anything once (but usually twice or three times). I seized any opportunity to get dirty and dusty. My poor mom would dress me in pretty girly outfits, and I'd come home caked in dirt like I'd been in a mud-wrestling match, not in a classroom. She also tied my hair into pigtails—no surprise I barely ever made it home with them intact. Hair was a big thing for my mom. As a child, she wore her hair short and hated it. No daughter of hers was going to have short hair! I had such long, thick hair that the ponytails or pigtails had to sit on the very top of my head so my hair wouldn't get in my way. At one point, I remember my hair was longer than my whole body! If I would leave it down, it would drag on the ground and get leaves in it. I hated when my mom brushed it, and she had to chase me around to get me to stay still long enough to work out the tangles. I would cry, and she used to call our old cat, Mickey, over "to get the rats in my hair." I would laugh, and suddenly the brushing felt a little more tolerable. But not much.

I brought my lunch to school in a lunch box in the shape of Mickey Mouse's head. Yep, Mickey's head opened up to reveal PB&J sandwiches, Capri Sun juice pouches, and Fruit by the Foot snacks. My other favorite lunch included a bologna, cheese, and mayo sandwich. I can still taste it today if I close my eyes. For a little snip of a thing, I always seemed to be starving. I loved eating cereal late at night—Cinnamon Toast Crunch, Cap'n Crunch, Apple Jacks. I poured ridiculous globs of Hershey's Syrup into milk and drank Nesquik chocolate milk by the gallon. I guess I burned all that sugar pretty quick and easy. Ah, youth!

I remember having the biggest crush on JTT—Jonathan Taylor Thomas from the TV sitcom *Home Improvement*. I listened to NSYNC and the Backstreet Boys, but my very first CD was the Spice Girls—I was totally Posh Spice! I loved watching Nickelodeon, *Hey Arnold!*, *Are You Afraid of the Dark?*, and Saturday-morning Looney Tunes cartoons. I was optimistic that Wile E. Coyote would catch the Road Runner at least one time. I was nuts about the Power Rangers and, of course, wanted to be the pink one.

I was always a whirlwind: hard to pin down and hard to convince that anything was unsafe. I was all about pushing myself to test my limits and defying what people expected of me (not to mention gravity!). The only time I "settled down" was for carpet time, the time when Mrs. Butcher gathered our class around her on a tiny rug to talk about something.

I loved, loved, loved Mrs. Butcher! She was small, about four foot nothing, with a warm, nurturing voice and a beautiful smile. I was captivated by her. I think I also loved just being physically close to everyone in that circle and checking their faces out and seeing their reactions (maybe this is where my love of people watching started). You can learn a lot about someone just from watching their eyes. I loved trying to figure out what made my classmates tick. I loved the idea that I could read their minds and secretly wished for that superpower.

I remember we had this little brightly colored playhouse in the corner of our classroom, and we could climb in, on, and through it. I was always playing and hiding in it, even when I wasn't supposed to. I also remember painting at the easel and all the colors and the water cups we'd use to rinse out the brushes. I loved mixing the thick, gooey paint to create new colors. It blew my mind when I learned that yellow and blue made green. Who knew?

I was outgoing and chatty. Blake, a cool kid with a long rattail trailing down his back, was one of my first friends. We met in line at kindergarten registration and stayed friends through high school and long after. There was also Ashley. I remember one time she went to Mexico with her family on a vacation and came back tan with her hair in tiny little braids with beads on the ends. *How amazing*, I thought, *to travel somewhere else in the world and come back changed by it.* It's funny how you realize things when you're writing a book and reflecting on your life. Even as a kid, I had wanderlust. Staying in one place—or one small town—was not in the cards.

I think most kids liked that I was fun-loving, adventurous, and always down for anything. I was also a talker. Basically, I never shut up. Every report card I ever got said the same thing: "Jen is so great, well-organized, uses her time wisely, works well with others . . . but she talks way too much in class!" I remember only one kid in kindergarten who didn't instantly take to me. One day, out of nowhere, a girl in the yard at recess pushed me out of my wheelchair. I landed hard on some rocks and just stayed there, staring up at her. Frankly, I was really confused and wondered, *Where did this come from? What did I do to make her so angry?* The answer was nothing. I had done nothing. She had experienced a rough upbringing and had a lot going on at home—I got in her way. It wasn't about me at all; it was about her. That taught me this valuable lesson: violence is seldom about the person it's aimed at. She was in pain and needed to lash out. I was an easy target. She should have thought twice about that beforehand though, because all my friends rushed to my aid and jumped on her like white on rice!

Imagine That

My body wasn't the only thing always in motion when I was a child; my mind raced as well. Once I mastered reading, I found a little place in our apple tree out back to squeeze my booty into. I'd climb up high, tuck myself between a few sturdy branches, and plow through book after book. Finishing one only fueled my desire to start another. It was my first "me time," where I learned how important it was to find moments and places to connect with myself and my thoughts. Later it would become my time to pray and connect with God as well.

My VIPs

My Kindergarten Teacher: Christie Butcher

I remember Jennifer on the second day of kindergarten. She came in the room in a wheelchair, and her parents left with the rest of the parents. Her eyes were wide as she looked around—not nervously, but in wonder. I had a little art center set up, and she had this beautiful little dress on. I turned around for two seconds, and when I looked back, she had moved the chair over and climbed up on it then on top of a little desk. I have no idea how she did all that, but she did! She was covered head to toe in paint and was happy as a lark! I thought to myself, *What do I do? What do I say? This certainly was not my plan!* But it was obviously hers. So I said, "Jennifer, what are you doing?" She looked at me with those big eyes and replied, "I'm an artist, and I'm making a work of art." I had to try to keep a straight face as we went over the class rules: we do things when the teacher says it's time—not when you do.

She was so strong-willed! She would take her legs off, and I'd ask, "Why did you do that?" Her response was, "Because I can run faster without them. They get in my way." People at the school wanted to physically change the building for her, to put in ramps and an elevator chair. Jennifer would have none of it. "Mrs. Butcher, no! I don't need it. I'm tough, and it doesn't bother me." That was the truth. She would come in with skinned elbows, and I'd say, "My goodness, Jennifer. What happened?" and she'd cheerfully tell the class she'd been roller skating the day before or playing softball. Bloody hands and elbows were a small price to pay.

She never saw herself as having any limitations, and I didn't either. She was bright, happy, helpful, and always interested and excited—Jennifer was the first to do anything, to try anything. She had that go-getter attitude, and her parents let her be who she was. There is something innate that pushes her forward—there always has been and there always will be.

I discovered The Chronicles of Narnia by C. S. Lewis and became hooked—I couldn't read those books fast enough and was drawn to the mystical creatures and breathtaking adventures. It was the idea of a foreign world that called to me, including magical, marvelous creatures that could fly and breathe underwater. And animals that could talk! *Why, I wondered, does it have to be fantasy? Why can't believing something is true actually make it that way?* I thought so hard about these imaginary scenarios, it made my head hurt! I tried to picture what I would look like with a mermaid tail or fairy wings. What if I drank a magical elixir like Alice from *Alice's Adventures in Wonderland* and it made me shrink or grow really tall? If I had Aladdin's magic carpet, who would I invite to take a ride with me (and would my brothers fight if I chose one over the other)? Did fairy dust exist like in the movie *Hook*—and how could I get some from Tinker Bell?

I was a little girl who got lost in these make-believe worlds because they showed me a realm where anything and everything was possible. They definitely planted seeds of curiosity. If horses could fly in Narnia, why couldn't I?

Fifth grade was a big year for me. My teacher was Mrs. Sweat. She had wild, curly brown hair with streaks of blonde and red, and she always had really long fingernails, so I loved the sound of her tapping on the keyboard: *tick-tick-tick-tick*. She carried her coffee cup with her everywhere, and it was stained with red lipstick. She buried her reading glasses in her epic hair most of the time, and she dressed uniquely. She had spelling bees in the classroom and always gave out awesome gifts as rewards for the winner (this was a good thing for me, because I was great at spelling). I have no idea why, but she let us sit on our classroom tables. Sitting on a table was something my mom never let any of us do at home—it simply wasn't polite. But Mrs. Sweat had no issue with it.

I met my best friend, Krine, that year. She was in Mr. Waldrop's class, the class I thought had all the "trouble-makers" in it. But it didn't seem to bother me. Krine was a bit of a wild child, and I was a Goody Two-shoes, yet we clicked. She also was adopted, so we bonded over that, though her grandparents raised her. The girl was a pistol (still is!). When she got older, she loved to party and always had the hottest boyfriends. I, however, was a quirky, funny, slightly uptight teen who lectured people not to smoke, drink, or sleep around. Like I said, the good girl. As Krine and I got older and became extremely close in high school, her confidence gave me confidence. She taught me how to bust out of my shell and not be self-conscious about anything. We were total opposites, and God gifted us with each other. We would talk and talk for hours, a lot of the time about my spiritual beliefs. Krine was never big on faith and was very vocal about it (as she was about everything), but I was equally vocal about how I felt about God. That's the thing I love about our friendship, even to this day. We can be 100 percent raw, real, and truthful about how we feel about something, even if we don't agree, and no one's feelings get hurt. But God worked on her heart through our friendship, and she eventually became a believer.

"I don't know where I'd be without you," she likes to tell me. But I honestly don't know where I'd be without her. She taught me so much, loved me so deeply, stood up and fought for me. God brings people into our lives to help us learn, not just about the world, but about ourselves. Looking back, I see that Krine gave me my first opportunities to speak about my love for God. She helped me find my voice. When I think back on it, we seemed the most unlikely duo—but God knew better.

Famous for the Right Reasons

Fifth grade was also my year to soar—literally. It was the first time I went on a plane. I was asked to be on *The Maury Povich Show* (before it got a bit more salacious). It was my very first time outside our little community speaking about myself and my life. I had been on local TV, and a film crew had been shooting a documentary about me for four years. But for *Maury*, I had to go to New York City, and the producers flew us first class and sent a white stretch limo to pick us up from the airport and take us to the studio. I felt like a celebrity! I remember being backstage, wondering why they were making such a fuss over me. I was twelve and didn't have a clue. I hadn't yet figured out that God had made me this way so I could inspire others.

— *My VIPs* —

My Best Friend: Krine McDaniel

Jen is not like the rest of us. She is from somewhere else, somewhere suspended in air, which makes her profession so fitting.

She always knew how to pinpoint happiness in her life and re-create similar moments. She didn't believe we needed eight-hour school days. It literally made her laugh to think we were there for so long each day. After we each got our driver's licenses, we would skip study hall and extend our lunch break by about forty-five minutes. We would drive to the next town, have great conversation on the way, then go to a Chinese buffet and eat and laugh until our extended lunch was over. That was happiness, and Jen created it. It was simple for her: "Do what you love with the people you love, and know that you are fortunate."

What Jen does physically is incredible. But who Jen is as a person and the way her brain works is what is really astronomical.

My mom went out onto the stage and talked with Maury, and then I came out. Maury asked a lot of questions, mostly about how I got to be so good at sports and tumbling. I chatted with him like he was sitting in my living room—I felt perfectly natural in front of a live audience and thousands of TV viewers. People ask me all the time how I learned to be such a good public speaker. I have always been able to do it with ease, and a lot of times, especially when I'm talking about faith and trying to lift people up, I feel like God is speaking through me. It truly is a gift I was born with. While my classmates stumbled and stuttered over oral presentations or stared down at their feet, I could wax poetic on most topics and look folks straight in the eye. Maury shook my hand; he was impressed. I was pretty poised for a little girl from a small town.

Then that was that. I went back home, back to being me. I made other TV appearances—one on the talk show *Arabella* in Munich, Germany, when I was thirteen, and I also gave interviews with newspapers and magazines all over the world. I was nervous to go to Germany at first because I'd never been outside of the United States and wasn't sure how foreigners would react to me. I remember people staring more than I was used to. It really bothered my dad, but not me so much. I was too excited about being somewhere new. But I do remember once we were in a German mall and a woman became so distracted staring at me that she almost fell down an escalator!

When I got back to school, some of my classmates were a bit standoffish, and I couldn't figure out why. I had always had so many friends, but now I felt like an outcast. After lots of frustration and hurt and talking to my mom, I realized they were jealous of the things happening in my life. One appearance led to another, and I was becoming something of a local celebrity. For a while my peers held it against me. I get it: I was doing things they'd never dreamed of. I was getting all sorts of attention and privileges. I understood why they were reacting the way they were, but that didn't make it hurt any less.

"I don't think I want to do this," I told my mom.

"If you can help one person and change one person's life, then it's worth it," she insisted.

I let that sink in for a while. *Why?* I wanted to know. *Why should I do this? Why does it have to be my job, my responsibility?* It wasn't until years later that I was finally ready to accept that responsibility and realize that I did have something important to say. I don't ever travel around holding microphones, being on stages, or performing in front of audiences because I think I'm "so awesome." I don't do it for the glory or the fame or the money. I don't tell people, "Here are ten steps to happiness. Just follow what I do, and you'll be happy forever!" That would be saying I have it all figured out—and I don't. I believe this is what I was born to do. The reason my roller coaster of a life has had so many interesting twists and turns and ups and downs is so I can share those experiences with others. The reason I've been given a platform is to share my heart, my stories, my passions, and my love in order to have a (hopefully) positive impact on others.

You too have talents, gifts, and abilities (I like to think of them as your personal superpowers) you were born with that are unique to you. They are equally as important—and abundant—as mine or anybody else's. The beauty of how God made us is that we don't have to be jealous of someone else's superpowers, because they weren't meant for us. This is one thing I would tell you to keep in your back pocket at all times: know that you are significant, you do matter, and what you have to offer is powerful. How powerful? Just like I do, you have a platform and an audience. Just think about the people you interact with every day: your co-workers, your family, your significant other, your kids. They're watching you, noting what you do and don't do. We all have an opportunity every day to have a positive impact on the lives of others in both big and small ways.

My mom has always kept a journal—stacks of them with every page filled. Every night while I was growing up, she'd sit in her chair in the living room and write away. Then one day she handed me a blank one of my own. "One day you'll thank me," she said.

Okay, Mom. Here's what you've been waiting for all these years: you were right. That journal became a place for me to write about my feelings and work out my frustrations. I wrote when I was ticked off at something and/or someone, when I had a crush on someone, when I was confused or afraid or simply lost. She knew the words would come easily, and I would never ask, "Why me?" I feel like God is the real author of this book. He's giving me the insight and the experience and the words to explain how and why He has shaped my life.

Writing a book was a choice I had to make, to allow God to take me to and through this place. God shows us the opportunities and puts them in our path, but we have to be strong enough to grab them and then hold on for all our worth. My family says I've always been stubborn as a mule, and I can't help but think maybe that's not such a bad thing after all.

BELIEVE IT!

God Has a Plan for You

Giving up control is not easy, especially for a control freak like me. But I've learned that the more I surrender and let God take care of things, the better off I am. I get out of my own way, I get out of His way, and then I let Him do His work. Because I have allowed Him in, I have more peace now than I have ever had in my entire life. I have given more and more areas of my life to Him, trusting that His plan and His way are *the* way for me. My dreams are laughable when compared with God's plans for my life! His gifts, ideas, and blessings are so much bigger and better than anything I could possibly imagine! All because I let Him drive and stopped trying to grab the wheel every five seconds. It was humbling to realize that I might actually not know what is best, even for myself. I am and always will be a work in progress: always teachable, always growing, and always trusting that God will never steer me wrong.

CHAPTER THREE

Can't Is a 4-Letter Word

Trust in the LORD with all your heart and lean not on your own understanding; in all your ways submit to him, and he will make your paths straight.

—Proverbs 3:5–6

I thought a lot about my future from my perch in my backyard apple tree. I've always been an old soul who likes quiet contemplation. I remember sitting up in that tree, listening to the sounds of the crickets chirping and birds singing and leaves rustling. I could feel the wind in my face and smell the scent of fresh-cut grass wafting in the air as the sun gently warmed my skin. Being so tiny, I also loved being up high, looking down on the world from a totally different vantage point. It was a place where I could breathe, where I could take in God's miracles without being distracted. I spent hours and hours in those branches, sometimes so relaxed and happy I'd fall asleep. As I grew older, it became my pondering place, a spot where I could read, write, and reconnect with my feelings. A place where I somehow felt closer to God, physically because I was high up and spiritually because my soul was so at peace there.

Clearly, I get my way of thinking—and my appreciation of the simple things in life—from my parents. They are blue-collar, easy-going, plain-living, salt-of-the-earth people who don't know how to take no for an answer.

My mom was one of eight children, the second to the youngest with four older brothers. She learned from a very young age how to wear many hats. She led a cooking, cleaning, sewing, grow-your-own-food, catch-chickens-for-your-meat-and-eggs type of childhood. She was taught to always work and provide for herself and her loved ones—laziness was not an option. One of her first jobs was working the line at the Heath factory, which is now the Hershey factory, in Robinson, Illinois. Her mom was a homemaker, and her dad worked at the local pottery factory. It was a true small-town Midwestern upbringing in the '50s—the stuff Norman Rockwell portraits are made of.

My mother had recently broken off an engagement to be married and was essentially over the idea of dating when she met my father. He was twenty-seven at the time, somewhat rough around the edges, and a looker. Like my mom, he came from a large family—he was the baby of eleven kids! He moved around constantly as a child, from one place to the next, because his dad liked to experience different places, and his mom followed suit. They landed in St. Marie, Illinois, where my dad went to high school and his dad owned a bar. My dad started working when he was just nine or ten years old and fully supported his family at seventeen. He was a "pumper," one of the men who checked the wells for Marathon Oil.

Both my parents wore a lot of hand-me-downs and did hard labor, but they learned the value of a strong work ethic and a deep love and appreciation for family. No matter what, family came first. This philosophy became the backbone of my childhood. Anything worth having is worth working hard for. Nothing can stand in your way if you have people who love you on your side. My parents always told me to be my authentic self, never to try to impress anyone or put on airs—just be who I am because that was the way God made me. My dad is rock solid and consistent. He doesn't care if you're the pope or the president, he isn't going to put on an act or be anything other than himself in his button-up flannel shirt and jeans. He'd give you that shirt off his back if you asked him, and I've never seen him pass someone stranded on the side of the road without stopping to help. Growing up with kind people like my parents for role models, I naturally developed a giving heart and an expectation that people should help one another.

As I grew up, I kept asking my parents, "What do you want me to do or be?" The only answer I ever got was "We want you to be happy." Come on, guys, give me a clue! Many of my friends' parents had strict plans and rules for them. Mine let me be me and make my own choices and mistakes. They gave me the power to have my own mind and my own dreams. They raised me to be strong and to stand behind my convictions. They had absolutely 100 percent faith in me, and that helped me feel the same way about myself. They let me be who *God* made me to be, not who *they* wanted me to be or thought I should be. They didn't believe in doing things because others did and never were impressed by money or titles or status. They were impressed by work ethic, character, empathy, honesty, and how you treat others. They never missed a sporting event, a school recital, or a church program I was in. Ever. Those things mattered to both of them. Family mattered. My brothers are the same way. They are very involved dads, braiding their girls' hair and painting their nails. Cooking. My parents did a great job raising all of us!

For the longest time, I wanted to be a veterinarian. I loved animals, especially dogs, and was set on pursuing this career until I realized part of the job was putting animals down when they were old or sick. I didn't have the heart. I could never kill a living creature. Then I thought I wanted to be a lawyer.

My parents always told me I was good at arguing, so I figured I'd be a natural. I'd seen the movie *Legally Blonde* and could envision myself before a jury being "legally brunette" and rocking a pink suit. Then I heard how many years law school is . . . *pass*! Patience has never been my strongest virtue.

My next career goal was fashion—either a personal shopper or a buyer or an editor for a cool Christian fashion magazine that inspires and uplifts women instead of objectifying them. I was going to go to a community college after high school, then fashion school. But God had other plans for me. For the record, I might revisit this goal one day down the road, because I believe someone should create a magazine without Photoshop and airbrushing that shows real women in a realistic light. I also thought I might be a shoe designer— how hilarious is that? I was obsessed with shoes and thought I'd be able to create some serious shoe art with wild and unique designs. My mom always jokes that she never could have afforded me if I could have worn shoes—the Brickers would be bankrupt. I am, however, a shoe enabler. Anyone who goes shopping with me is not leaving the mall without buying at least a few pairs.

Living without Limits

Sometimes the only thing that could get me to come down from my perch in my tree was to tell me the Olympics were on TV. One day I was completely absorbed in the gymnastics competition when I turned to my parents and announced, "I'm going to be an Olympic gymnast when I grow up." There was a brief pause, then they nodded. "Wow, okay," they said. To them it *was* okay. They would never dissuade me even if the idea seemed far-fetched. I used to think they were pretty crazy, but now I realize they were always ten steps ahead of any wild plan I could dream up. They always saw the potential in me. They always believed I would live an extraordinary life that defied all odds. They taught me how to look past my circumstances. They taught me to be brave, for which I will be forever grateful. A life without fear is a life without limits.

I was six years old the first time I saw Dominique Moceanu on TV. It felt like a lightbulb went off in my head: *Aha! I want to be like her.* She was tiny; I was tiny. She was fiery; I was fiery. She was born to Romanian parents; I knew I was born to Romanian parents. We even looked alike, with the same tan skin, huge dark eyes, and thick jet-black hair. I was drawn to her but couldn't say why. I remember a poster in my gym of the Magnificent Seven, Dominique's 1996 US Olympic gymnastics team, and one of her on the beam. I told myself, "One day, that will be me."

I'm not sure what it was about tumbling that appealed to me, but I do know I was always attracted to activities that required strength, technique, and focus. I also loved the speed and sensation of flying across a room. I felt like I had been shot out of a cannon. From the time I was in second grade, the gym at Beth Allen Power Tumbling was my second home. At that time, the gym was in Newton, which was about twenty minutes away from my house. I didn't complain though, because there was a Hardee's on the way, and I got to eat hot ham-and-cheese sandwiches (they used the white cheese instead of the yucky orange cheese, which made me so happy) on the way home. I might have loved those sandwiches as much as I loved learning how to power tumble. I wasn't in that building long before Beth moved her business to a gym that was conveniently located by my school. But no more ham-and-cheese sandwiches!

When my mom first called Beth, she explained my fascination with gymnastics and asked her if she'd take me on as a student.

"Sure, we can try," Beth said. "But honestly, I've never helped anyone like that. Let's see what she can do."

I wanted to do it all. My very first day, I did a forward roll. I had such drive and passion for tumbling, there was no stopping me. The gym had a Tumbl Trak, one beam, some floor mats, and a long rod spring floor that we competed on. Between the track and the rod floor were rainbow-colored mats where we would practice handstands, cartwheels, and round offs. We used to have handstand contests to see who could hold a handstand the longest. Big surprise, I always won! I could stand on my hands for hours if I had to. When it came to tumbling, I didn't need as much of a running start as other kids—why waste time when I could just get down to it?

"I want to do a back handspring," I told my coaches one day. I could tell Beth was a little unsure. It was not an easy move, even for a kid with legs. But I was determined and wouldn't even let them spot me. I never let anyone spot me for the longest time, and I'm not sure why. I just wanted to take on the challenge all by myself, to prove to myself I could do it without anyone's help. Looking back, it was crazy—I could have killed myself! But I was strong-willed and stubborn. I hated feeling needy.

I remember I also didn't like my mom watching, so I would ask her to leave, especially when I was working on something new. I was pretty hard on myself. If I didn't perfect something immediately, I would pitch a fit. My coaches, Beth and Karen, always had to remind me that I was human.

"Practice makes perfect," they'd tell me. But I wanted to be perfect right out of the gate. If they said I did something well, I didn't accept that either. I had to feel it was good, and not just good for *me*, but good for any able-bodied gymnast.

My biggest challenge was getting the height other gymnasts with legs could achieve. As my skills grew, height became exceedingly important for mastering the more complicated moves. I couldn't get the height on the rod floor to do a full rotation of a full twist, and it was holding me back from going up in levels. But I never allowed anyone to give me special treatment—ever. I just stayed at the level I was at because I didn't want to advance by having people make exceptions for me.

Most of my fellow athletes accepted and respected me. I had only one incident in the four years I competed. One of the girls I competed with called a meeting with her mom and the coach. She didn't think it was fair that I was placing higher than her—how could that be possible when she had legs and I didn't? Legs or no legs, I was just better than she was. But she and her mom didn't want to hear it. Also, audience members occasionally stared at me when they saw me on the sidelines, but for the most part, everyone was extremely positive and encouraging. When people did stare, I didn't notice them too much. I was too focused on the competition.

I had a pretty tough shell back then, and like a turtle, it protected me. But I eventually realized you can be so tough that you block out everything and everyone. If you accept only perfection, then that becomes the sole thing of value in your life—and there's so much more than winning. Letting

– *My VIPs* –

My Power Tumbling Coach: Beth Allen

The first time I met Jen, I thought, *Oh, what a cute little doll!* She was always happy—one of the happiest kids I have ever met. Bubbly, willing to try new things, kind to everyone, a team player. The first time she came to the gym, I didn't know what was possible to teach her without legs. And to be honest, I was constantly worried when she learned new skills. Even when she did it by herself, I would watch with one eye and say a prayer. *Please don't let her hurt herself!* But she was not a bit afraid. She didn't want help—even though I made her accept it. She did it all so easily. It was in her—the gift and the talent were there.

She had a very strong drive to learn more and do well. Basically, our approach was to experiment. We had no idea what to expect or what she could do physically. We practiced on the Tumbl Trak and *nothing* scared her. She

my guard down and accepting that I'm flawed are things I've had to work at. God meant us to fail. It's His way of helping us accomplish something far more important and lasting than a momentary victory. It took me years to learn how to focus on what's been given instead of what's gone. But now I realize that the victory is in the journey—even if I stumble along the way. Thankfully, I had parents who understood that. Who let me try and fail and try again. When my belief in myself wasn't strong, theirs was stronger.

I hope that one day when I have my own kids, I can demonstrate a similar strength for them. All parents have a hard scared me sometimes, but she was so confident. To teach her I had to think about what it would be like to *be* her and how I would compensate for not having legs. Then we could figure it out together.

When she competed or practiced, everybody in the gym would stop and watch. They weren't staring; they were admiring her. At meets she would often get standing ovations. People were shocked at her power and mesmerized by her. Coaches would come up to me and say, "I tell my kids on my team when they're whining and complaining, look at that little girl who doesn't have legs. Look at how hard she works and what she can do." Everybody knew Jen. When she came in fourth at Junior Olympics, I was so happy for her and her parents—it was so deserved. They are such beautiful souls, and I was so proud of and thrilled for all of them.

I didn't know what Jen Bricker would go on to do with her life after tumbling—but I knew it would be tremendous. And I was right.

time seeing their child unhappy, frustrated, or down on themselves. My parents had trust in both God and me. They resisted the urge to jump in and rescue me. Instead, they let me figure things out for myself. They let me find my own courage and wisdom. They let me fall on my butt. All were equally important. No one wants to lose. No one wants to be in last place. No one wants to fall. But God is our safety net. And in His eyes, we fail only when we allow failure to defeat us, when we refuse to trust that failure can be a gift—a chance to be better, stronger, and smarter the next time around. God uses everything in our lives to transform us into the people

He wants us to be. Maybe that's why I never let anyone spot me—I knew He had my back.

BELIEVE IT!

You May Be Your Own Worst Enemy

I was always incredibly self-critical. My parents would plead with me, "Jennifer, don't be a sore loser. Be a good sport!" when I didn't come in first place at a competition. I wish I knew then what I know now: self-critical thinking is truly self-sabotage. I get it—succeeding and winning feel good. Losing or failing . . . not so much. But cut yourself some slack. Have compassion for yourself. Try to offer yourself a little love, understanding, and acceptance. Everyone has their bad days. It doesn't mean you're a loser or your situation is hopeless. Manage your expectations. Are you being fair to yourself? It's great to have huge dreams and goals, but are they attainable at this point in time? Do you have a lot of work to do before you get there—or are you trying to skip a few steps? And finally, savor the small victories. Are you appreciating the little things you've accomplished en route to the bigger goal? The first competition I won might not have been the Junior Olympics, but it was preparing me for when that day arrived. When was the last time you truly stopped and appreciated how far you've come instead of bemoaning how much farther you have to go?

CHAPTER FOUR

Sticks and Stones

Whoever claims to love God yet hates a brother or sister is a liar. For whoever does not love their brother and sister, whom they have seen, cannot love God, whom they have not seen.

—1 John 4:20

When I was five, I attended the wedding of my cousin Jody, and an adult wedding guest asked me, "Why don't you have legs?"

I paused for a moment to consider, then I put it into the simplest terms I could think of: "Well, you know when sometimes someone takes a Polaroid picture and it just doesn't develop? That's what happened to me."

My parents said they were blown away by my answer and had no idea how I came up with it. It was the perfect explanation (and the perfect way to silence someone so nosy). But, frankly, I would rather people ask than make assumptions. Assumptions are almost always wrong and are fueled by ego, ignorance, and even fear. So go ahead, ask me anything! I can take it. I know people often have preconceived notions about me. For example, they think, given my circumstances, that I must have been a bullied kid and that I'm surely an unhappy adult with limited abilities. They think I need help opening doors (for the record, I don't, but I've learned to accept the gesture with a smile). They think they have to tiptoe around the fact that I have no legs (yeah, I kinda know that already). Here's the thing: I am happy, and I am strong (wanna arm wrestle?). I had an amazing childhood, and I don't mind talking about the fact that I don't have legs. I'm not offended. There doesn't need to be an elephant in the room. I'm a big girl (okay, technically small), and I've heard it all before.

And as I've grown older, I've learned a valuable lesson: the way you react colors the way people react to you. If you lose control of your emotions, then you're admitting they've won—they've gotten to you. But if you keep your cool and don't let them push your buttons, then who's winning? That's power. A lot can be said for owning who you are. When you're okay with yourself, people are put at ease. Do people sometimes say stupid things? You better believe it. I've lost count of how many times someone has said something inappropriate to me, but they do so almost always out of misunderstanding or ignorance. I view it not as a personal attack but, rather, an opportunity to educate, enlighten, and open someone's mind and heart.

I was visiting New York City recently and called for an airport shuttle to take me to John F. Kennedy International Airport. I travel the world extensively, so I'm kind of a pro at the routine: getting in and out of vehicles with my luggage and wheelchair, checking in, going through security, boarding the plane. None of it fazes me. In fact, I've been in so many airports that I rarely need to look at a map or any of the overhead signs to find my gate. So when I got into this particular shuttle, I thought it would be just another ride in traffic out to the airport. No biggie. Instead, it turned into a huge scene. The driver took one look at me and launched into a tirade.

"They didn't tell me about *you*," he said, as my friend helped me load my things into the van. He looked me over, top to bottom, and made a face. "They should've sent a handicapped van!"

The word *handicapped* felt like a slap in the face. No matter how I tried to explain that I was perfectly fine and perfectly capable of simply putting on a seat belt, he continued ranting about "the handicapped girl" and saying he shouldn't take me. As if I were a thing, not a person, in front of an entire van filled with passengers. No matter what I said, no matter how fiercely I defended myself, he kept going. I could feel the anger rising in my body, and eventually, I simply lost my cool. It was so embarrassing, so degrading, so wrong. I don't really remember what I said, but it wasn't pretty. Finally, we got on our way, but the driver was muttering under his breath the entire ride. I was mortified and outraged at the same time.

When I got to the airport, I was physically shaking with rage. My skin was actually hot to the touch. I called my friend Grant and told him what had happened. I was fuming, not just at this stranger's ridiculous and insensitive comments but at my own reaction to them.

"You're always the one telling me that everything happens for a reason," he counseled me. "Take a deep breath and try and find the reason."

I sat waiting for my flight, going over the incident again and again in my mind. Then I started writing. I poured my heart and my fury out onto the paper. And when I reread it, I no longer hated this driver for hating me. I felt sorry for him. And I knew I had to put this story in my book. I called Grant back. "I'm not the first person this has happened to, and I won't be the last," I told him.

But I might be the first to put it out there. To make people aware, so that if they witness injustice and prejudice, they say something. They don't allow people to be victimized

– *My VIPs* –

My Uncle: Gary Bricker

I came to watch Jen play shortstop on her Little League softball team. She took her teammates aside and gave them a pep talk: "Look," she said, "I know we always lose, but my uncle Gary came all the way from California, and he didn't come here to see us lose!" I remember watching her round those bases—man, was she moving! She made it all the way to third. Of course, they won. Jen has always been a motivator—and a person who speaks her mind.

Another time, I was sitting on the sofa and Jen crawled up next to me. She was about six years old, and she kept staring at my argyle socks. "You're looking at those like you don't like them very much," I teased her. She said, "Well, I don't hate 'em, but I certainly wouldn't wear 'em!" That was diplomatic!

She would call me all the time, and we would talk and talk for hours about anything and everything. Her phone bill must have been atrocious! But she always had a lot to say—and so much intelligence for a little girl. No question she would grow up and do great things, none at all.

for being different. This goes for not only someone like me ("disabled") but also people of different races, religions, colors, backgrounds. Nothing burns me more than someone judging others.

God is the only Judge. James 4:12 says, "There is only one Lawgiver and Judge, the one who is able to save and destroy. But you—who are you to judge your neighbor?" I was pretty mad that day, so I wasn't about to go tossing Scripture at some guy who hated his life, his job, his whatever, and decided to pin it on me. You can't control what people will do and say; you can only control your own actions. Just know that God is watching. He sees their behavior, and He sees yours.

Not Such a Small World After All

After high school, while many of my friends went to college, I decided I would go into the college program at Disney World in Orlando, Florida. At the time, I was still determined to go to fashion school, so this seemed like a great way to get some work experience, make some money, and get out of my tiny little town and assert some independence. I loved my community, but I was outgrowing it. I couldn't see myself living there for the rest of my life; that felt suffocating to me. I was biding my time at Lincoln Trail College, a community college in Robinson, the next town over, when I happened into a bathroom stall and saw a flyer for the Disney College Program. Interviews were being held at a college about thirty minutes away. I took that as a sign, went on the interview, and two weeks later (which seemed like an eternity) received an acceptance letter in the mail. I was going to Disney World!

It was a fifteen-hour drive to Orlando, and my brother Bubba and my dad helped me make the move. My parents didn't stand in my way—they knew I needed to figure out how to be on my own. I was nineteen, and I had never cooked for myself or washed my own laundry! The program was supposed to be from January to May 2007, but after about the first month, I realized I was never moving back to

Illinois. I knew from a very young age that I was going to live in a big city—a small town couldn't hold me. I extended my program until August. It was amazing—there were so many people from countries all over the world. I had never even heard some of the languages being spoken. I worked at Disney's Hollywood Studios in operations, but the job included a lot of hospitality. I worked parades and made sure people didn't cross the lines or run out in front of a float. I also worked the *Fantasmic!* show, loading thousands of people in and out of an area the size of an enormous baseball stadium. During the day, I would help people plan their day, get their bearings. If someone was lost, I pointed them in the right direction. I used to play this game with myself: guess where the guest is from. I got really good at it, just from looking at them. I could tell what country they were from based on their sneakers, their haircut, and how short their shorts were.

I loved to socialize and was quite the party animal, staying up till 4:00 a.m. every night, hanging out with my fellow students. I never drank, but I did talk . . . and talk . . . and talk. And one night, I met this cute guy with a great smile. We were chatting, dancing, flirting, and he asked if he could walk me out to my car. When we got there, I could tell he was struggling to say something. I was thinking to myself, *Dude, spit it out!* when he finally did.

"You're just . . . ," he began. "You're just too pretty not to have legs!"

I burst out laughing. I almost felt bad for how hard I laughed in his face. He was attracted to me and confused about how to handle the situation and how to verbalize his thoughts. I get it. And I took it as a compliment, not an insult.

Disney was an eye-opener for me. I guess I had never realized what people outside of my town would think of me. One day when I was greeting guests, a woman came up to me. "Wow, good for you!" she said, practically patting me on the head. "You've got a job! You're out there working!"

My jaw dropped. I wanted to say, "And what would you expect me to do? Hide in a dark room because I don't have legs? Dig a hole and crawl into it?" But I held my tongue. I tried to smile politely (I was, after all, working at the happiest place on earth!), and then I wished her a good day. Visitors constantly shared condescending comments—at the very least, I heard a few each day—but I couldn't say what I was thinking. Disney had some pretty strict rules about how we were supposed to treat guests. "You're an idiot!" wasn't in the handbook.

And I thank them for that. It was a great education for me in how to cool my temper and not take everything so personally. It was also a reality check: *Jen, not everyone is going to love and appreciate you like they do back home.* I was a stranger there. I looked different from what people view as "normal." I had to deflect a lot of simpleminded, snarky comments and just let them roll right off my back. People so often speak without thinking.

A Weight on My Mind

God knows, I'm not wholly innocent myself. For a time I had a real prejudice against overweight people, and I'm very ashamed to admit it. But it's something I need to get out in the open because I don't ever want to portray myself as perfect or a saint—and I don't want people to think it's okay to do what I did. The blind assumptions that have been aimed at me I once aimed at others. I used to see people who were overweight as lazy, out of control, and selfish. My reasoning went something like this: If you don't like how you look, then freaking *change* it. Don't whine about it! Don't tell me you "can't," because I don't buy it. I couldn't change that I was different; no amount of diet or exercise or self-control was going to change the fact that I didn't have legs. But the way I viewed it, people who were overweight *chose* to be that way.

Then I started watching a TV show called *Drop Dead Diva*. In a nutshell, a young, blonde supermodel with a gorgeous, tiny, rockin' body dies and comes back as a plus-sized lawyer. The character, Jane, first freaks out at what she looks like. But then she grows to realize she is still the same person on the inside. At her new size, she is an extremely powerful and brilliant lawyer. She makes tons of money, has her own assistant, and drives a cool convertible. She dates handsome, intelligent men and has a fulfilling life. She isn't sad or lazy or less of a human being in any way. Her revelation became mine as I watched the show through all six seasons. Then I discovered the reality show *Extreme Weight Loss*, and it all clicked. These people were suffering. They had been through tragedies or frustrations in their lives that were overwhelming; being overweight became their armor. Every week I watched and cheered for them. I became emotionally invested in their stories. I rooted for them. It takes a huge amount of courage to face your demons head-on. I envied them—that's true heroism.

What I came to realize is that I have no right to criticize *anyone*. I don't get to make assumptions based on appearances. I certainly don't like it when people do it to me and should know better. Everyone—no matter what they look like—deserves God's love. We all come in different "packages," and that shouldn't define us. People are not their circumstances, situations, failures, accomplishments, regrets, or mistakes. They are not their color, their height, their weight. People are people. We all have hearts. We all have emotions and feelings. We all crave love, acceptance, and forgiveness.

I guess when I was hating on overweight people, I was acting more like that shuttle driver than I'd care to admit. But we all, at our core, are just human beings, capable of messing up not once, not twice, but over and over again. When we make assumptions—and we all do—we fail to recognize how our personal beliefs and prejudices are coloring the way we think. So why do we do it? Because it's easy. Because it feels real even when it's not. Because we tend to see and hear what we want instead of what's true. People make assumptions because they don't have the courage to ask questions or to try to understand. We think we know one another, but we never truly give ourselves that chance. When we judge others, we miss out on the opportunity to connect. And that, to me, is the greatest tragedy of all.

BELIEVE IT!

Haters Gonna Hate—
You Don't Have to Take the Bait

I will never apologize for being who I am or doing what I love. Whenever you follow your passion, you can bet people will judge you, stand in your way, or make you feel bad about your choices. They will watch and wait for you to mess up so they can jump in and say, "Told you so." Or when something great happens, they will rain on your parade and try to make you feel unworthy. Usually, these types are not bad; they just lack meaning in their lives. They resent you for feeling fulfilled when they feel so empty. For this reason, I don't get mad when people hate on me. I know it's not about me; it's about them. I take the higher road. Think of yourself as Teflon. Nothing—especially nasty comments—can stick to you. And respond with love. There's no need to argue or prove anything. Instead, be kind, compassionate, and calming. It's possible to change hatred into love, negativity into positivity, envy into friendship. It all starts with understanding. Haters need love, but their bad behavior gets in the way. Look past it and respond with an open heart. Sometimes that small gesture is all it takes to turn someone from being against you to being on your side.

CHAPTER FIVE

Keeping the Faith

But when you ask, you must believe and not doubt, because the one who doubts is like a wave of the sea, blown and tossed by the wind.

—James 1:6

My mom says that when I was young, maybe five, I told her very matter-of-factly, "I'm gonna live in a city, and I'm gonna be famous." I don't remember saying that, but she thinks I must have had a vision. I had to have known it somehow.

I also knew at ten years old that God had a huge plan for my destiny. I didn't know what it was, but I knew I was going to change the world and help people.

I don't remember a time when my family didn't go to church—it was an essential part of my life and my upbringing. When my parents first adopted me, they threw a huge baby shower in the Hardinville Christian Church basement so friends and church members could meet me. My mom is a mighty believer. She grew up going to church, and she's witnessed God move in her life. She's seen prayers answered and dreams come true (that would be me!), and her faith is iron strong. Without faith, she tells me, without trusting God, life is void and meaningless.

I do believe that. My life without God would feel empty—like a huge hole in my heart and soul. You can try to fill that hole all you like, and people do. They fill it with drugs, alcohol, food, money, unhealthy relationships. Have you ever wondered how to fill the emptiness you sometimes feel? What do you reach for? Who or what do you turn to? What I've learned is that God fills you up with joy, peace, wisdom, gratitude, hope. God is the only reason why anything in my life makes sense. The only reason I have anything is because of Him, and I know that without His guidance, I'd be a train wreck, a hot mess. I know I'd be broken. He is my strength, my perseverance, my clarity, my perspective. And I owe so much to my parents for putting those wheels in motion. They introduced me to God's greatness. They opened the door.

Everyone in Hardinville went to one of two churches. Ours was right beside our house, so we could walk over. We had a couple different preachers during the time I attended there. Pastor Joe Putnam and his wife, Lois, served for several years and were really good friends with my parents. When I was five years old, I had these red-frame glasses with no lenses that I insisted on wearing to read. My mom called them my Sally Jessy Raphael glasses, and I did look a lot like the talk-show host when I wore them. I guess I thought they made me look serious and scholarly. Lois led the singing in church, and when she told us to get out our hymnals, I piped up, "Wait! I need my reading glasses!"

The church was so small, just big enough to accommodate the twenty or so people who came to Sunday services. I remember there were mainly older people—very few kids—but it didn't bother me. I liked grown-ups. I held my own among them. I can still picture the rows of pews with green cushions and a place to get baptized to the right of the stage.

My parents and my church taught me to love and fear God—but not like He's some big bad wolf. God is good. He keeps His promises. In return, we honor Him with our respect and reverence. He commands us to live a certain way and calls us to follow Him and give up our own selfish desires of the flesh if they are not in alignment with His will. But everything He commands is for our good, to set us up for the best possible life. I didn't always understand that as a kid. I thought there were too many rules and lessons to follow. It felt overwhelming. *How could I ever live up to God's expectations? How could I ever be so perfect?* As I grew older, I realized God doesn't want perfection. He simply wants us to try our hardest, and He forgives us when we don't measure up. He wants us to have a relationship with Him. When you get to know Him better, you get to know yourself better. You see yourself through God's eyes.

My parents taught me that God is above all, and He is to be honored and respected. He is the reason we prayed before meals. He is why we prayed at night before going to bed. We thanked Him for the day and asked Him to protect us. I remember my mom teaching me the words to the prayer "Now I Lay Me Down to Sleep." I would be in some pink, frilly nightgown, next to her at the side of my bed, palms folded together, eyes closed, reciting:

> *Now I lay me down to sleep.*
> *I pray the Lord my soul to keep.*
> *If I should die before I wake,*
> *I pray to God my soul to take.*
> *If I should live for other days,*
> *I pray the Lord to guide my ways.*

That prayer has more to it, but that was about all I could remember as a child! My mom taught me to bow my head out of respect for God and all He has done for us. She told me that angels were always surrounding me and protecting me. I envisioned them as magical creatures dressed in white,

– *My VIPs* –

My Friend: Courtney Grant

The first time I met Jen was in the Orlando airport. It's a long story, but in a nutshell, I was her new roommate who moved in when she was out of town. Her other roommate, Nick, had asked me to come along with him to pick her up. From what I hear, she wasn't all that thrilled about having me as a roommate. I didn't have a job or a car, and she said, "Oh no!" But I won her over, and we eventually lived together, all three of us, for more than a year.

Jen is the only person (besides her family) who calls me Grant. It's how I introduced myself to her—I had an agent at the time who thought it would be a better name to use while I was modeling. Now I'm back to Courtney, but to her I'm still Grant, and that will never change.

flying around with wings and maybe playing harps. I now see them as warriors. They protect me. They defend me. They vanquish my enemies and my obstacles. I have no doubt that angels watch over me—I've seen them in action. I've felt their presence when something could have gone horribly wrong but didn't.

In preparation for Easter Sunday services, my mom would take me shopping for a new dress at the mall, and we'd pick out something pretty, usually with lots of ruffles and lace, though one spring I switched it up and did navy blue with white polka dots. One year right before Easter, I decided to cut my hair into a bob just below my ears. Because everyone

She always can make me laugh, and we are best friends. There isn't a day that goes by that we don't see, call, text, message, or Snapchat each other. She'll go away on a long trip for work, and I'll say, "Bye, have a good one." She'll get all angry at me. "Why aren't you sad? Why don't you miss me more?" And I'll say, "Gee, Jen, I know you're going to send me a message the second you get to Dubai or Japan or wherever you're going!" We're that connected. It's not like an ocean or a few continents are going to keep us apart.

Over the past eight years we've known each other, we've grown so much together. I think God has a huge plan for her life. She's someone people are just drawn to because of the energy she puts out there. You can't explain it. It's just Jen. She's the most giving person, and when she wants you to be a part of her life, she is all about it and all in. I love being on the receiving end of that.

freaked out so much, it was the first and last time I sported a short 'do. My long hair is my trademark!

Learning to Celebrate God

I started going to Camp Illiana, a church camp, in sixth grade. It was a little more than an hour away from home and just across the Indiana border outside of Washington, Indiana. The first time I went was amazing: an entire week of epic worship music, singers, and guitar players. They sang the coolest worship songs, like the ones I'd heard on the Christian radio stations, filled with passion and conviction. As I and the rest of the campers sang along, we raised our hands in the air, literally swaying to the music. I'd never seen people worship this way. People at my church were pretty mellow and just sat there during services. They didn't rock it out! I felt very uncomfortable at first, but then I found myself forgetting to be self-conscious. I let the music and the words fill my soul, and soon my hands went up in the air.

The camp was secluded and small, but to me it seemed immense. You had to go up and down huge, steep hills throughout the property to get to the cabins or to worship or to eat. I would look up at the trees scraping the sky and notice the sunlight peeking through them. It felt so safe and peaceful there—shut out from the rest of the world. I also loved all the great activities: we had two pools, an epic zip line through the woods, a giant swing, kayaks, canoes, even a rock-climbing wall. It was heaven for this crazy little tomboy!

After going to camp and experiencing worship and sermons in such an empowering way, our tiny church back home didn't make much sense to me anymore. It just didn't have that passion and fire and emotion I felt should be part of how we celebrate God. I told my parents in eighth grade that I wanted to go to a different church. The Highland Church of Christ was also in town, and they went on mission trips, had a worship band, and sponsored youth conferences. My parents said they would take me to Highland, but they'd still go to Hardinville Christian Church "with the rest of the old people." Eventually, I got them to come with me, and they switched over as well and are still members there.

When I was thirteen, I attended a huge Christian youth weekend conference in St. Louis. I had the most awe-inspiring worship experience, almost like a rock concert because there were about two thousand of us. I was just one in an enormous crowd, but all of a sudden, I felt like the worship leaders were speaking directly to me: "If anyone is feeling led to get saved, you are welcome to come down front here. We'll pray with you and for you!"

The last thing I wanted to do was go in front of all those people—it would be completely humiliating. But, out of nowhere, I was hit by a wave of emotion. I started crying—and I do not cry. Ever. Especially not in public! Yet I couldn't stop. Then I felt like I was being pulled to the front of the auditorium, and I couldn't fight it. I went up and made the decision to be saved, right there and then. It was a powerful, spiritual, God-filled moment in my life. I can't tell you what the catalyst was, just that I was ready. God got through to my heart at that moment, and it was the first step in my spiritual growth. I was baptized two weeks later back home in my church. It was my decision entirely, a commitment I wanted to make.

My relationship with God continued to grow throughout my teen years, but there were constant distractions (namely, friends and boys!). I always felt like God was waiting in the wings for me whenever I needed Him. He waited patiently and never got annoyed if months or years went by between one of our long, heartfelt talks.

When I moved to Florida after high school, I found an absolutely amazing nondenominational church called Real Life. The preacher, Justin, was in his late thirties at the time. He wore a plaid button-up shirt and jeans, and usually flip-flops. He had a bit of a Southern accent and was just a good ol' country boy who kept it real. This church was alive and on fire for God! During every sermon I was transfixed and transformed. I walked away profoundly changed, and it felt like my eyes were being opened to a whole new understanding of God and what it *really* meant to be a believer. It takes strength. It takes devotion. It takes an unwavering commitment to live your life how God wants you to live it.

I joined a young adults' group *and* a women's group that met weekly. But three days a week of Jesus time still wasn't enough for me. I was learning so much and meeting so many new people, it was almost like church camp again. There was just one big difference: we were all now dealing with grown-up life. I was living on my own, paying bills, struggling with relationships. I needed God more than ever, and I felt like I'd been away from Him far too long. I was ready to stop being "lukewarm" in my faith. I wanted to practice what I preached and be accountable for my actions.

One of the most remarkable people I met during this time was my friend Kelly. I was attending a Sunday service one morning, sitting in the back because I was new and didn't know anyone. We started talking and then sat with each other every Sunday after, eventually moving up to the front row. Kelly had a faith like I have never seen before. And she was living her faith, not just talking about it. I loved watching her worship: her eyes closed and her hands lifted high toward heaven. After church every Sunday, we'd go to lunch and talk about the sermon and the rest of our weeks. It's rare in life to find someone who is pure through and through, who walks the walk and doesn't just talk the talk. When I think of her, I can hear her saying, "Yeah, girl, you got this!" She always reminded me of how beautiful and talented she thought I was and how proud she was of me. Because of Real Life and Kelly, I started getting more serious about my prayer life and

— *My VIPs* —

My Pastor: Jeremy Treat

From the minute you meet Jen Bricker, you find yourself asking, "Where does she get such strength?" Jen will be the first to tell you that it's her faith in Jesus. And as her pastor, I can tell you that her faith is legit and that she lives her life as a showcase of God's love and grace. As much as Jen has accomplished, her identity is rooted not in what she has done to inspire others but in what God has done for her in Christ. I love the fact that my four young daughters look to Jen not only as an amazing gymnast and a woman who has overcome obstacles but also as someone who keeps her eyes fixed on Jesus. God's grace is shining brightly through her, and I praise God for that.

reading the Bible, always striving to read every morning and pray every morning and night. I felt like I was growing closer to God, getting to better know and understand Him—and myself as well.

When I moved to Los Angeles, I had a bit of a tough time. My apartment was bare except for my laptop, a cot for a bed, and a collage from my friend Mariana that she made for my going-away party in Orlando. I only knew a few people, and everything in LA was bigger, harder, and more expensive. I prayed to find a strong Christian community of friends and a church that was as great as Real Life. It took me several years, but I finally landed at the church I'm at now, Reality LA. Hands down, it is the most exceptional and unique church I've ever been to, and 100 percent the answer to my prayers. Reality holds three Sunday services in a big high school auditorium. It's primarily a millennial church, meaning worshipers are all in their twenties and thirties. The pastors are real, vulnerable, open, and honest people. During worship, all the lights go dim on- and offstage, so there is no distracting from the Word of God. I've learned that His Word is a living word, and it speaks to us on so many different levels every time we read it. For me, the same verse can apply to something totally different on a different day. Little by little, I'm making my way through the Bible in its entirety, but not just for the satisfaction of checking it off my to-do list. I am searching for its meaning, its light, its significance to where I am and where I'm going. My faith has grown because I've seen how God has showered me with His blessings. Honestly, I get a spiritual high from prayer. It lifts me and grounds me at the same time. It constantly reminds me that I am never alone, never unprotected, never unloved. And that is a blessing in itself. Even on my darkest days when I am feeling discouraged, desperate, or just plain ticked off at someone or something, it's my life preserver, pulling me back to safety.

BELIEVE IT!

You Have a Calling

I pray every day, several times a day. It doesn't take long, and it doesn't take much effort. God doesn't expect you to give Him an entire oration! Just open your heart and speak what's in it. For me, praying instantly brings me back to my purpose and connects me to Him. It's a feeling of instant peace and calm. *Jen, you don't have to worry, you don't have to stress. God's here. He's listening. He's got your back!* If you're out of practice, don't worry. You don't have to kneel or even close your eyes. You don't have to crack open the New Testament. Just let your heart do the talking, and God will get the message loud and clear.

Ephesians 2:10 says, "For we are His workmanship, created in Christ Jesus for good works, which God prepared beforehand so that we should walk in them" (NASB). I believe this. I believe God made me the way I am so I could get people's attention, so I could spread His Word and make a difference in some small way in the world. It was no accident—not fate or chance or circumstance. God doesn't make mistakes. He has a particular plan in mind for each and every one of us. Knowing that empowers me and helps me embrace my calling.

A lot of people tell me, "Good for you, Jen. You know your calling. I don't have one." I say you do, and even if you have no idea what it is just yet, God does. Some people are born knowing what their calling is, while others need to discover it over time. It may not be revealed to you overnight or even for several weeks, months, or years, but it's there. You may have many callings in your life—some big, some small—but they all are important. They're helping you become the person God intended you to be. Try, fail, and try again. Be okay with not knowing what you're doing. Be okay with looking silly or feeling awkward. Be okay with putting your trust in God and knowing He'll always be there for you. It's like having your own personal cheering section always chanting, "You can do this!"

Need inspiration? Think about what makes you smile, laugh, feel exhilarated. What would make you want to leap out of bed in the morning and start your day? What would get you off the couch? Think about it: Where do your heart and your happiness lie? Maybe it's something you loved doing as a kid. Maybe it's a hobby. Try to embrace it. Don't worry if it's not the same passion your friends or family have. God meant for you to be yourself. He gave you your own unique gifts. Who wants the same wrapping paper on all the presents under the tree? Not me! I want diversity—different bows, a variety of sparkles, and many colors. If we all had the same passions, the world would be pretty boring and dull. When you do what you love, you are fulfilling not only your own needs and desires but also God's plan for your life. That's a win-win situation across the board!

CHAPTER SIX

Breaking Down Walls

Be strong and courageous. Do not be afraid; do not be discouraged, for the LORD your God will be with you wherever you go.

—Joshua 1:9

I couldn't resist doing a handstand in Dubai in front of the beautiful Burj Al Arab Hotel.

A candid shot captured while rehearsing on set with Heidi Latsky Dance in NYC.

Taking in all the beauty overlooking Aspen, Colorado.

Kangaroo-pouch
style with Dad!

All my friends on the
playground with me.
Ah, the good ol' days!

Up to bat in a softball game
in third grade.

Bouncing high in the backyard with my
brother Brad.

Little me at almost a year old.

Birthday party with Granddad.

Morning snuggles with my brothers and Dad.

My parents came down
to my going away party in
Orlando, Florida, in 2010.

My family celebrating my parents' 40th
wedding anniversary.

One of very few pictures taken with my prosthetics and my brothers.

With my cousin Zach
at a family wedding.

I love big presents!

Posing in my prosthetics.

Getting a picture with all my brothers actually behaving is quite a feat. Love these guys!

When my worlds came together—brothers and sisters.

Eating at one of my favorite spots here in LA with my sisters.

Twinning with my little sister Christina.

Celebrating with my sisters at Christina's baby shower.

First time Nick Vujicic and I met.

Me and Grant all fancied up at the Shane's
Inspiration annual gala in 2013.

Just hanging around with my
rigger Ray. He's *the best*!

Posing with my friend Amanda outside
a beautiful mosque in Abu Dhabi.

In the middle of the Arabian Desert, Easter 2013.

Speaking in Abu Dhabi, the capital of the United Arab Emirates.

Snuggling with my camel friend on a desert safari in the United Arab Emirates.

Kneeboarding for the first time in Dubai.

Performing at The Act in the Shangri-La Hotel in Dubai with my amazing friend Aaliyah.

Learning how to fly in the wind tunnel with the Inflight Dubai crew.

Handstanding in the bamboo forest
in Kamakura, outside of Tokyo.

Mid-flip during rehearsals
in Tokyo, Japan.

Speaking to this massive audience in Hong Kong was such a thrill.

Scuba diving in
Costa Rica with
my friend Mike.

First time surfing in Sydney,
Australia.

Overcoming my fears in
Sydney, Australia, holding a
Burmese albino python. Her
name was Jenny!

Sightseeing around Sydney,
Australia, during the Britney
Spears tour.

Flipping around at XMA here in LA.

Performing my signature move in the city that has made my dreams come true.

Performing at the Hollywood
Roosevelt Hotel for the Shane's
Inspiration annual gala.

Handstand pic with
the Tokyo Tower.

My first speech at a graduation ceremony, right here in LA. What an honor!

Enjoying the sights and sounds of Niagara Falls.

Speaking at a large high school outside of Salt Lake City, Utah. Those kids were awesome!

Posing in my very first yukata (a summer kimono) at the Tokyo airport.

I climbed down some crazy cliffs to capture this shot in Hawaii. It was definitely worth it!

Speaking at Capital Christian Center in Sacramento, California.

The first rule of tumbling is that you need to stick the landing: feet together, standing strong and tall without wavering or taking a step. Of course, this was virtually impossible for me. My body automatically "bounces" as I complete a tumble. I needed to figure it out: How could I stick my landing and not get points deducted from my score? My coaches and parents considered talking to the judges and agreeing on some kind of special allowance. But I was determined: no special treatment. I would do the same thing that every other gymnast in my competition category did. We came up with this way for me to sort of "sink down" at the end of the routine and hold that position—my version of sticking it. It required the same strength and concentration as someone holding their legs firm, so it met the criteria.

No matter what sport I competed in, I always determined that to win a medal or a trophy, I had to earn it. I put in the same blood, sweat, and tears as everyone else competing, and no exceptions were made. Did it hold me back from advancing? Maybe. But to me, that was better than someone accusing me of having an unfair advantage (a few competitors did that anyway). It was never about the actual win for me; it was about proving that nothing is impossible.

My coaches saw I was a talented power tumbler. I had a natural sense of body and air awareness. And I was strong! I had defined biceps and triceps from the time I was five

— *My VIPs* —

One of My First LA Friends: Valerie Remy-Milora

I met Jen shortly after she moved to LA, and she immediately became family. Over the last few years, I've been blessed to witness the beautiful ways in which Jen touches everyone around her.

I first witnessed this with my youngest daughter, Sabrina. She was a little over two when Jen came into our lives. My daughter was delighted to meet an adult who was her size and loved to laugh and play as much as she did. When they first met, they talked for hours: laughing, riding in Jen's chair, just having a wonderful time together. Sabrina had all sorts of questions, and Jen answered every one of them with a smile.

On the way home, Sabrina sat quietly for a while before thoughtfully announcing, "Mom, I want to be like Jen. I

years old. About a month into fourth grade, Beth asked me to start competing on the gymnastics team. Fancy leotards with sparkly stripes down the arms! Team jackets! I was so excited to be part of this world. During competition season, my team would drive every weekend to a different city or state for a meet. I would do two different "passes" utilizing different skills, such as half twists, backflips, tucks, and round offs.

When I showed up at a meet, people would, of course, notice that I didn't have legs—and I don't think they understood I'd be competing. How could I? But after a few meets, I became known not just for my lack of legs but for my skills want to cut my legs off!" My heart skipped a beat. I took a deep breath, pondering how I would answer, and then I realized the infinite wisdom of this precious child. Sabrina wanted what Jen had—she wanted her passion, her joy, her love of God, and her love of life! She wanted to dream big and live a life filled with one awesome adventure after another. She was a child who saw no obstacles because Jen did not show her any.

And that is one of the greatest gifts Jen shares with all of us: she gives each one of us the opportunity to be like children again, to look at the world around us as a place filled with wonder and exciting opportunities. To anticipate each day and know that something special is going to happen—today, tomorrow, and the day after that. And to believe, without a shadow of a doubt, that everything truly is possible. That is the most beautiful and priceless gift anyone can receive!

and sociability. I was always friendly and curious. I wanted to know where the other competitors were from, what their team colors were, their favorite moves. I was always full of questions about everyone's life!

When I participated in the Illinois power tumbling championship, I competed against competitors with legs. No one without legs had ever made it so far. One of the news media outlets said I was forging new ground as the first "handicapped" person to compete. I never thought of it that way though. I was simply doing what I loved to do, following my passion as far as it would take me. I see now that God put me here on earth to pave the way for many different people. I

think He proves numerous points and busts countless stereotypes through me. But I wasn't conscious of this for a long
time, especially not when I was a kid. I went all the way to
the AAU Junior Olympics, where I placed fourth all-around
in my division. For me, competing fueled my fire—not the
idea of being "the first" in anything.

Breaking the Rules

God's path for me has been filled with obstacles and road-
blocks. I'd be lying if I told you I've tackled each one with
grace. Some have tried me to the point of fury and exhaus-
tion. Some still do. Because of who I am, how I look, how
people perceive me to be, I know there will always be walls
to break down. I learned that lesson very young. When I was
in fifth grade, my parents took me to a theme park about
an hour and a half away from our house. I was so excited!
Everyone in my family was a roller-coaster junkie, and I'd
never been on one. I'd been waiting and waiting for that day.
We piled into our car and took my friend Kara along. When I
remember the day, it's as if I'm watching it play back in slow
motion: getting out of the car and rolling up to the ticket
booth in my wheelchair, then climbing out and strapping myself into this pendulum-like ride that pitched you around in a
circle.

I pulled down the harness and watched the guy running the
ride watching me. I saw a look of panic in his eyes. Then he
got on his radio and called someone else over—his supervi-
sor or a park manager. They whispered, they stared at me,
they whispered some more. At this point, since the ride was
going nowhere, I had a hunch I was the cause of the holdup.

"I'm sorry," he said, walking over to my row of seats. Kara and my entire family were strapped in next to me. "You have to be a certain height to ride this ride."

Translation: "get off." I get that the guy was doing his job and following the park rules, but the rules were wrong. To make matters worse, I had to make my way back through a long maze of people waiting in line. I felt as if each one was looking on me with pity.

My parents exploded. They were livid, more livid than I've ever seen them in my life. "How dare you!" my dad said, getting right in the guy's face. I was afraid he was going to punch him, but I was so upset that I didn't want to hold him back. "Are you kidding me?" he shouted at the employee. "You don't know who you're talkin' to!"

We were now all making a huge scene. But no matter how hard any of us argued, pleaded, sobbed, there was no budging the park staff. They offered to let my family and Kara ride—just not me.

This made my dad even more furious: "What is she supposed to do?" he screamed at them. "Sit there and watch us?"

In the end, they gave us back our money, and we left in a huff. The only rides they would allow me to go on were the ones for toddlers. I couldn't even go down a waterslide.

"They don't know you," my father tried to reassure me. "They don't know how strong you are and what you can do—or they'd know how ridiculous these rules are."

I sat silently in the backseat, trying not to cry. My mom was doing a good enough job for both of us. I was just so disappointed and stunned. All my life, I'd never accepted the word *can't*. Now here was someone telling me "you can't," and there was nothing any of us could do about it. It shook me to my core. Had my parents been wrong all along? Were there some things in my life that I would never be able to do?

The way my parents handled it next was spectacular. We could have sued. We could have alerted the media and made a huge stink. We could have played the handicapped card. Instead, my mom got on the phone with our state representative and told him, "There are laws that are wrong, and we need to do something about them." She called OSHA, the Occupational Safety and Health Administration. Then she got on the phone with theme park after theme park, educating them. In order to meet the height requirement for a ride, I would have to strap on prosthetics that would not be safe on a high-speed thrill ride. The safety belt would hold me just fine at the height I was at, and if they were so worried, they could add a second harness to reinforce it. I wasn't the only one missing limbs who wanted to ride a coaster. Why should anyone have to miss out?

Fast-forward about a year later, and we were all welcomed at Indiana Beach Boardwalk Resort amusement park. My mom had reached out to the owner, and he personally escorted me into the park and onto my very first roller coaster. I screamed with joy and rode every terrifying ride to my heart's desire. But not every amusement park is this way. To be honest, most aren't. I write this in the hopes that others will educate themselves and voice their objections to rules that don't apply to all people equally.

Every time I go to a theme park, it gives me anxiety, which is so ironic. Isn't it supposed to be a place where people cut loose and have fun? For me, it's a stressful mental and emotional exercise. I have to arm myself with patience. I have to be the bigger person and swallow my pride every single time. I also have to use my knowledge rather than lose my temper. I understand why the laws were made and how they work, more than any park manager, owner, or employee.

Not too long ago, a manager at a major theme park proceeded to explain to me why medically I couldn't go on a ride. "It will be impossible for you to hold yourself on the ride," he said, trying to sound very astute. "It has to do with your balance and equilibrium."

I took a deep breath. *Dude, you better stop talking. You have no idea what you're talking about.* I wasn't even going to waste my time and tell him that I can "balance" and "hold" myself thirty feet in the air from a silk just fine, thank you. I spin at lightning speed during my performances, and my equilibrium is just dandy!

Instead, I marched right past him, into guest services, and phoned OSHA. They set him—and everyone else who worked in the park—straight. After two hours, the staff escorted me back to the front of the line, and I got on the ride. A lot of time was wasted when I could have been enjoying the park instead of arguing with the staff, but I won. Unfortunately, I always have to be prepared for a fight—the intellectual kind. And it can be exhausting, but it's well worth it. I'm fighting not just for me but for everyone who has been told "you can't." Common sense is gone because people are so afraid of being held liable.

I think back to that day in fifth grade and realize my dad could have simply said, "Jennifer, the man said no, so no it is." Plenty of my friends grew up being told "rules are rules" and not to challenge authority. But that's not how my parents raised me. I was raised to be fierce, to fight the good fight nobly and with conviction. Today you may not win; tomorrow you may not win. But down the road will be one small victory that can change everything.

BELIEVE IT!

You Need the Right Team to Support Your Dream

I have a fantastic support team of family, and friends I consider family, who would do anything for me. My team is essential. I depend on these people to lift me up, give me wise advice, and even slap me upside my head if I need a little wake-up call! This group includes my parents, my brothers, my sisters, my friends Garry and Jason Clemmons (identical twins), Grant, Krine, my old roommate Cody, and my friend Hunter Allen. Hunter is an extremely calming person, and it's okay for me to be a mess, a wreck, not perfect around him.

Seek out these types! Look for people who have your best interests (as opposed to theirs) at heart. Friends who understand your hopes, dreams, and goals and will do whatever it takes to help you reach them. Fill your life with folks who make you want to be a better person. People with big, kind hearts and strong moral character. Choose people who push you. By this, I mean those who don't let you sit back on your laurels or get lazy. Instead, they empower you and remind you to take chances, try new things, venture out of your comfort zone. And finally, surround yourself with positive people. No naggers, worriers, or Negative Nellies. Choose people who see the glass as half full and encourage you to do the same. Whenever I am down, I immediately call or text someone like this, and they can point out the good in any bad situation. It's hard to be depressed or angry when you have someone assuring you that this too shall pass, and if it doesn't, there's always Netflix and ice cream.

CHAPTER SEVEN

Secret Sisters

A new commandment I give to you, that you love one another: just as I have loved you, you also are to love one another.

—John 13:34 (ESV)

A lot has been made of the story of how I reached out to my sister, Olympic gymnast Dominique Moceanu, and told her I was her long-lost sister. She wrote about it in her memoir. We talked about it in newspapers and magazines and TV interviews. But it's really just half the story. To me, the most important half is what came after that initial meeting: how my relationship with both my sisters and my biological mother has evolved. The story isn't over, because we're just finding our way in one another's lives.

I always knew I was adopted, and that fact didn't trouble me much. My parents knew eventually one day I'd get curious and start digging, but they hoped it would come later rather than sooner. My adoption was supposed to be closed; I wasn't even supposed to know who my birth parents were. But God was working overtime. He made sure that the social worker made a clerical error and gave my parents all that information. He knew one day I would need to reach out to Dominique.

That day came when I was sixteen. My friend Kassi was adopted and had found out her biological last name. It seemed so cool and mysterious—a piece to a puzzle. Could I find out mine? What would that reveal about me? I had never been curious about it before, never had any reason to think my parents were holding anything back. But God put the idea in my mind. It was time.

"So," I said to begin the conversation with my mom. "Do you know what my last name was when I was born? Do you know anything about my birth parents?"

Her reaction was kind of like *Hold that thought!* as she went to call my dad and ask him what to tell me. Should she wait until he got home from work? Should they tell me at all when I was still so young? He told her not to keep me waiting any longer—so she didn't. She pulled out a manila envelope filled with papers.

"Now, Jennifer," she began. "You're never gonna believe this." She laid out on the table all the documents she'd kept. "Your biological last name is Moceanu."

I knew. I just knew. On some level, I had always known. I think she was waiting for me to have a reaction but I didn't.

— *My VIPs* —

My Lifelong Friend: Kassi Wampler

I have known Jen since I was about ten months old. Our moms are lifelong friends, so we grew up together. We did all the things "normal" kids do: we swam and played sports, went roller skating, danced. Jen has always been a fun-loving, strong-willed, and independent person. We have so much in common. We are both the baby in the family and were both adopted. We have shared a lot of our lives together, and I know that for me, personally, having a friend like Jen has made my life a little brighter. I may not have been blessed with a sister of my own, but I have the next best thing in a great friend whom I have always thought of as one.

On the outside I must have seemed eerily calm, but inside I was freaking out. "Dominique's my sister." It was a statement, not a question. It all made sense now. My parents, of course, had put two and two together several years ago. While watching the Olympics with me, they saw the fourteen-year-old gymnast I was fixated on—and the names of her parents, who were watching in the audience. My mom had seen their signatures on my adoption papers. She knew at that moment my idol was also my sister.

But they made the very difficult decision not to say anything—not just yet. They didn't think it would be fair to either of us. I respect their decision and know it came from the purest of places in their hearts. Do I wonder what would have happened if I had known sooner? Sure. We missed out on a lot of years that we could have been living as sisters. But like I said, on some level I think I did know. I just needed it confirmed, and I needed to be ready to hear it.

Armed with my new knowledge, I went into detective mode and did some research online. I wanted to understand how I was born in Illinois when Dominique was born in LA. The answer was that my birth family had moved around the United States so that Dominique could train with different coaches. Our younger sister, Christina, was actually born in Tampa. I started to make sense of it all. When I went on Dominique's website and saw a picture of Christina for the first time, it was like I was looking at a photo of myself. *So that's what I'd look like if I had legs!* My dad walked by and quickly glanced at the picture on the screen. "Jen, when did you go skiing?" he asked.

"I didn't, Dad. That's my younger sister." She could have been my twin—not even my father could tell us apart.

I knew I had to get in touch with Dominique, but it wasn't as easy as picking up a phone. It took four years and several failed attempts. First, I asked my uncle Gary, a former private investigator, to find and reach out to my biological parents. He did talk to Dmitry and explained that I wanted to contact my sisters. Dmitry wasn't very receptive, but he did admit that he and Camelia gave a child up for adoption. After that initial conversation with my uncle, he was silent, making it clear that he wanted to keep the secret (me), and he wasn't going to help me contact my biological sisters. Failed attempt number one. So I switched my game plan and planned to contact Dominique instead. I subscribed to her website and saw she was on a gymnastics tour—and one of the stops was Indianapolis. That was only two and a half hours away from my home, so I had the genius idea to show up at the meet, get down to the gymnastics floor, find Dominique, and tell her I was her long-lost sister! It was the "perfect" plan in my head, but about two weeks before I was going to buy the tickets, I found out that she was injured and had to pull out of the tour. I was so bummed and discouraged! Failed attempt number two.

That was a low point. After my high school graduation and my big move to Florida, I was so overwhelmed and distracted that the idea of finding my sisters got put on the back burner for a bit. But toward the end of that year (2007), my thoughts and even my dreams became consumed by the idea of meeting my biological family. It was clearly God telling me to try again! So I gave it one third and final shot. I called my parents and told them I wanted to try again. I needed them to copy all the legal documents from my adoption and send them my way. Then, I called my uncle Gary and asked him to track down Dominique's address in Ohio for me. I copied pictures of myself from when I was a baby all the way to my current age, then crafted a carefully written letter that took *forever* to get just right. I made the decision to leave out the detail about me having no legs—maybe that would be a bit much to find out at the same time she was learning she had a long-lost sister. Finally, I packaged up my heart and soul in a big manila envelope and sent it out on a hope and a prayer.

In retrospect, the scene I made at the post office was pretty hilarious. Because Domi was famous, I was concerned about someone intercepting the package. I asked the postal lady about all of these hypothetical scenarios. "Okay, so if she isn't there, no one else can sign for her, right? And if someone is there and it's *not* her, they can't take the package, right?" I asked the same thing in different ways over and over again to make sure all my bases were covered and I hadn't forgotten anything. The lady must have thought I was nuts.

I waited for two weeks, truly the longest two weeks of my life. I remember I was talking to my neighbor at my front door. "I'm going to go check the mail," she said. "Do you want me to grab yours too?" I said, "Sure, thanks." She returned with a Christmas card. When I opened the envelope, a letter signed with Dominique's signature fell out of the card. In that moment, my heart stopped. I hadn't been waiting on this for only two weeks; I had been waiting and praying for four years. Then I was seized with fear. *What if she and Christina reject me? What if they don't want to have anything to do with me?*

It was one of life's true "Band-Aid" moments. Like ripping off a Band-Aid, it's best to just get it over with. There was no point in hesitating; I just had to get on with it and read the note. I'll never forget when I got to the middle of the letter and read Dominique's words: "You're about to be an auntie!" I knew right then and there that she had accepted me into her family. The next day there was a knock at my door and a delivery guy handed me a flower arrangement. *Who would be sending me flowers?* Then I read the note: "Love, Dominique and Christina." I knew Dominique was getting ready to have her first baby and finishing up college, so I decided to give her as much time as she needed. I let her take the lead. And I still have the vase the flowers from my sisters came in next to my bed on a nightstand. It marked the beginning of us finding one another.

A couple of weeks later, I was on my way to work at Disney when I got a call from a number I didn't recognize. I answered it and heard a soft voice say, "Hello, Jennifer? This is Dominique." I was so surprised that I didn't know what to say at first (I know—me, speechless! Shocking!). But really, what do you say when your childhood idol turns out to be your biological, long-lost sister? And then that sister calls you when you're not expecting it? I took a deep breath, tried to forget the awkwardness of the situation, and just talked like I would to a close friend. The conversation flowed so naturally that before I knew it, we had been on the phone for more than an hour. Toward the end of the conversation, I realized I still hadn't told her I didn't have legs. I was hoping that maybe her parents had filled her in about the reason why they gave me up. *Maybe*, I thought, *I'll just squeeze it in real quick, very casually . . .*

So that's just what I did. Right before we got off the phone, I said, "Oh, you probably already know, but I was born without legs." Dominique was pretty quiet on the other end of the phone for a minute. *Okay, so she didn't already know.* I could tell she was trying to process and respond in an appropriate way.

Then she kind of stammered. "Oh, oh . . . wow, no, I really didn't know that." She was trying her best to be polite and kind and not sound completely freaked out. I almost felt bad because she had already had one huge surprise (me!), and now she had to cope with another one. It was the reason I had purposefully left it out of my letter; it would have been way too much new information to handle at one time.

"So," she continued, "when can we meet? We all have to meet!"

It was a huge relief knowing that she wanted to get to know me. Four months later, in May 2008, Christina and I both flew to Ohio, and all three of us met for the first time at Dominique's home. At the time, our father, Dmitry, was still alive. But he died of cancer later that year. He knew the three of us were meeting, and I wondered how he felt about that. I was told that at the end of his life, he made amends with his whole family and even told my sisters he wanted to meet me. Unfortunately, he died before that ever happened. I had a million questions to ask him, and I think we would have gotten along just fine. Like me, he had a strong personality and was very driven. My sisters say he was proud of me, of "the Moceanu" in me. I think at the end of his life, he realized and regretted the mistakes he'd made. I hope he found peace and took comfort in the fact that God is good and wanted our family to finally be whole.

Though my sisters and I wanted things to go smoothly and easily, we each needed to go through an adjustment

– *My VIPs* –

My Sister: Dominique Moceanu

Within minutes of meeting Jen, you get a great sense of who she is. She has a personality bigger than life: very bubbly, very outgoing, a great sense of humor—we can always joke, always laugh. I appreciate her drive because I had a lot of that when I was growing up—and still do today. She has set her mind on a goal, and she's working toward all her big dreams. I see that while growing up she got to be a child and blossom and become the person she is today. It's amazing what that kind of childhood can do for a person, what love can do.

She's gotten much stronger and closer to God in the time I've known her. We talked about that a lot at our last visit; it is great to have reached such a comfort level that we can talk about anything. I'm much more private with my faith. I'm proud of my faith, but I've chosen to be more private about it over the years.

period. I had to figure out how I fit in this family that was so different from the one I grew up with. I was the outsider, the new kid on the block. Domi and Christina had a rough childhood during which they learned to rely on each other. As a result, they're always going to be closer, and I have to be okay with that. I'll admit I was a little jealous at first. They had inside jokes. They had memories. Christina struggled as well—she had always been the little sister, and now she had to share that role and let someone else in. The only way to grow our relationship was to invest time

I try to be careful not to be too much of a big sister. Jen's strong-willed and strong-minded. I'm there for her when she needs guidance. I know she wants to go through and figure things out on her own. I'm always here for her to bounce ideas off of, and I love our conversations. I always want to give her advice, and I want her to feel like she can come to me when she needs it. But I also want to give her space.

She's on a path toward her big goals. She's living her dreams. I'm just excited to be part of the journey. In two more years, we will have known each other a decade, which is crazy when you think of how our relationship began. I'm proud that our relationship has never been forced; it has been a natural process that gets better over time. We're probably at the best place we've ever been as sisters as far as our comfort levels go. There's been much healing that has taken place over these past eight years, and it's been a great emotional journey that we've both grown from.

in it—talk things through, be open and honest with our feelings.

Time is the key word. After Dominique and I were in contact with each other, another four years passed before we shared the news with anyone beyond our small, intimate circle of family and close friends. We couldn't talk about it publicly. We waited for many reasons, but most importantly because Dominique felt we needed time to get to know each other before fielding an onslaught of questions and media attention. I was frustrated, but I understood. We each needed to process the situation in our own way. I had to miss Christina's wedding because people couldn't know about me yet. Then, in June 2012, Dominique's book was published, and she and I did an interview that aired on the TV show *20/20*.

It was a bit melodramatic! Some news sources called our story "shocking," "a dark family secret," "a sin of omission." They characterized Domi's life as "tumultuous" and my letter to her as "the biggest bombshell" of her life. She admitted that rage was her first emotion, then denial. She felt like her life had been a lie.

Hearing our story told was surreal. We all knew the story, but seeing it on national television was an entirely different experience. Once the story aired, my phone blew up with people asking me, "Why didn't you say something?" So many people in my life didn't know. I remember driving in LA the night the *20/20* piece aired and feeling like a huge weight had been lifted. And being able to post that first picture of all three of us on Facebook was a huge moment.

Meeting My Biological Mother

I met my biological mother for the first time in 2009 in Dominique's home in Ohio. I remember the phone rang and my heart did a backflip: Camelia and her husband were about five minutes away. It felt like the scene was happening in slow motion. I heard her come through the door, speaking words in Romanian I couldn't understand, and then she entered the living room. She had on this huge fur hat and walked toward me slowly. I held my breath.

She hugged me and kept speaking in Romanian, so Dominique had to translate. She said how much I looked like Christina and Dmitry. Over the course of the afternoon, I showed her videos of me performing with Britney Spears and pictures of my acrobatic and aerial routines. She was proud of all the great things happening in my life. She told me she knew she never could have given me any of them. I sensed a great deal of sadness even when she smiled. She seemed haunted by a past that she had little to do with and that I don't hold her responsible for. But no matter how much I assured her that I was fine, that my life was happy and I was healthy and everything was good, she couldn't forgive herself. It's something I can't do for her, and I know it will take time. But I also know she's a woman of faith and that will get her through. She believes in God, and He'll help her realize she's not to blame and this was always part of His plan for me.

My parents came the next day to meet her as well and brought a shoe box full of old baby pictures. I have always wondered if they felt uncomfortable during those early re-unions, but they supported me 110 percent. If they were nervous or worried, they didn't let that get in the way. They put my needs above all else and trusted that although I was getting closer to my biological family, they wouldn't lose me. Our bond is way too strong.

We all had dinner together that night at Dominique's. As I looked around, I realized that both my worlds were com-ing together at one dinner table. Isaiah 55:8 says, "'For my thoughts are not your thoughts, neither are your ways my ways,' declares the LORD." God's plans are so much bigger and more impressive than ours. His goal for your life is more rewarding, more fulfilling, more spectacular than you've ever dreamed possible. The trick is staying open to those possibili-ties. Let God in and let Him work His wonders.

BELIEVE IT!

Life Isn't Always Black and White

Sometimes life can be really colorful and complicated, and things you never could have seen coming in a million years just *happen*. What then? You have to adapt. My pastor said something one Sunday at church that has stuck with me: never put anything past yourself, and never say "never." You may think to yourself, *I would* never *do this* or *I would* never *do that*. But the fact is, we are human and we make mistakes. This is why we need to show grace, compassion, empathy, and forgiveness. Everyone's path is different. Everyone has different struggles, challenges, childhoods, joys, triumphs, defeats. We cannot fully relate to one another because we will never walk another's exact path. I've made mistakes, I'm not perfect, and I've done things I'm not proud of. But I've also shown forgiveness. I know life isn't always simple and clear-cut, and we can't judge someone for doing what they do. That's between them and God. The only person you can hold accountable is yourself.

CHAPTER EIGHT

Sky High

I urge you to live a life worthy of the calling you have received. Be completely humble and gentle; be patient, bearing with one another in love.

—Ephesians 4:1–2

I was working in operations at Disney World in 2007 when I first saw *The Lion King* show at Animal Kingdom. I was obsessed and would sneak back in to watch it at least once a week. The dancers, the colors, the movements—the show was intoxicating. And it put an idea in my head.

Up until this point, I had wanted to be only an athlete. But something about seeing this show lit a fire in me. I thought, *I want to perform like that*. And once I set my mind to something, I get fixated on making it happen. Through a friend, I met Nate Crawford, a seasoned acrobat, gymnast, and coach who performed at Disney. We met up at a gym and started bouncing around together on a trampoline. He was enamored with all the possibilities of what I could do—and what we could do together.

"We should team up," he said, just like that. "Put together an act."

I agreed, but most of his friends warned him against partnering with me. They said it was "career suicide." He didn't tell me any of this right away. Frankly, he didn't care what people said. He went with his gut.

My gut, however, turned out to be one of our biggest problems: I was so out of shape! I hadn't competed in gymnastics in about five years and had virtually no strength, stamina, or definition. I had abs of flab instead of abs of steel! I needed to tone up, lose twenty pounds, and mentally prepare to perform. But exercising, especially cardiovascular exercise, is not easy for someone who doesn't have legs. I did it mostly through circuit training, kayaking, and jumping on a trampoline with Nate.

Nate was open-minded from the very beginning and confident he could teach me. He had traveled around the country performing with a professional troupe for ten years, so he knew what he was doing. He was full-on ready to take the "challenge" of teaching me to do what he did. He introduced me to the silks, red flowing fabrics straight out of a Cirque du Soleil production. I was totally enthralled by their beauty and fluidity, and also by the physical demands of working with them. Almost every trick Nate had ever learned was dependent on using his legs. He really had to get creative and figure out how to teach me everything he knew—without depending on his legs.

The first skill I learned on silks is called a "roll-up." You wrap the fabric on each hand around your wrist once or twice, lock your arms, hold yourself upright, and if you have legs, go into a "pike" position with your legs straight out in front of you and roll forward. Essentially, you're doing a front flip, and each time you flip, you roll higher and higher up the fabric as the fabric rolls higher and higher on your arms. This, of course, takes extreme upper body strength, as well as tremendous core strength. It also plays a trick on your brain, because every time you flip forward you feel like you're falling and want to bend your arms to catch yourself, but you can't. You have to get outside your head and trust the technique of the skill, never letting your elbows get above your shoulders and keeping your arms straight the entire time.

During the first month of learning this skill, my arms were purple, then black and blue from my elbow to my shoulders. A few people even stopped me in public to ask if I was being abused by a boyfriend! Doing just one roll-up seemed impossible and extremely painful. Then I would see Nate bust out six or seven, and I'd get mad at myself for being such a wimp.

"You're gonna do it one day," he told me. "Sooner than you think."

His belief overrode my doubt, and I sucked it up and did it. Little did I know, roll-ups are a skill for *very* advanced aerialists, and usually men—not women—do them. No wonder it was so painful and difficult! In hindsight, I'm glad Nate taught me one of the hardest things first—it gave me a huge amount of confidence. If I could do *that* skill, I could do anything. After a while, my body got used to the pressure of the tight fabric and I stopped bruising. I went from one to two roll-ups, and eventually, I conquered six. Then it was the battle of making it consistent. There's so much technique involved: move to the left or right and you become uneven, rolled up higher on your left or right arm.

Nate kept saying, "It's just numbers, it's just numbers," meaning the more times you do it, the more it becomes ingrained in you. Now I can proudly say I can consistently do five or six roll-ups every time. I don't even think about it. It just comes naturally.

Finally, we were ready to perform—but the world wasn't as receptive as I'd hoped. People were afraid of how audiences would respond to seeing me, a "handicapped girl," doing an aerial act. Every time Nate and I tried to book a gig, we got a lot of people saying, "Well, *I* like it, but I don't know how other people will react." I knew audiences would go nuts and love it. I knew they'd forget the minute I went up in the air that I didn't have legs. I also knew it had never been done before.

In the Spotlight

Our first performance together—and my first performance *period* in the entertainment industry—was in the Mascot Games at the Amway Arena in Orlando. We performed our high-energy and highly technical trampoline act. The opportunity came up at the last minute when the main act for the halftime show canceled, and they needed a replacement ASAP. So two days before the event, we got a call that we were going on. I was a nervous wreck: five thousand people would be in the audience! Couldn't we start smaller? We went into the stadium the day before to rehearse, and everyone involved with the event was there, including the head honchos who had hired us. I grabbed Nate's arm in a panic. *What if they take one look at me and change their minds?*

"Don't think about it," Nate said. "They need us." He was right; we were in a good situation. They were totally desperate and had no other choice. The minute we finished our rehearsal, everyone started applauding. *Okay, they aren't going to change their minds. This is really happening.*

Right before the performance, I was physically shaking. In all the times I'd competed as an athlete, I was calm, cool, and confident. Sports? Gymnastics? I knew I had that in the bag. But this was the stage. I was going out there as an artist. Then the lights dimmed, and out we went on the trampoline. I got in "the zone," trusted Nate, and tried not to look out at the thousands of faces staring at us.

When we finished, the entire stadium erupted into thunderous applause. I don't think I stopped smiling for hours afterward. And Nate? Totally pumped—and a little relieved.

The first silks performance Nate and I did was with Heidi Latsky, an unbelievably talented and innovative dancer and choreographer, and the artistic director and founder of Heidi Latsky Dance. Heidi had heard about us and asked us if we wanted to collaborate. She was working on a project that involved both able-bodied and disable-bodied dancers/performers. It was a lot for me to digest. I had never done any

– *My VIPs* –

Artistic Director and Founder of Heidi Latsky Dance: Heidi Latsky

During my first phone conversation with Jen, I fell in love with her because she told me she was terrified to work with me. Modern dance was out of her comfort zone. But that was the very reason, she said, that she *had* to work with me. I was struck by her candidness and openness, and her willingness to take a risk. In all the years we have worked together, these very same qualities have permeated her relationship with me and my company. She has been the consummate professional and a complete joy to work and partner with. She is a brilliant talent and a shining beacon of optimism. I have often told her how much I wish I had that positive outlook she has in abundance. I am so proud of what we have created together and of our profound friendship.

dance before—let alone modern dance—or worked with a choreographer. I also had some hesitation about being portrayed as "disabled" and performing for that community. Nate spent a lot of time trying to talk me into it and, ultimately, he did. He convinced me there was a ton to be gained in going outside my comfort zone. Dance without legs? Sure, why not?

In retrospect, working with Heidi was one of the best decisions I have ever made. She taught me how to pull emotion out of my heart and replicate it on stage, how to block out everyone around me, and how to truly connect with my partner. We ended up creating a mesmerizing twenty-minute silk routine—which is unheard of. The most performers do on silks is five to six minutes. We performed it first in Albuquerque, New Mexico. We had this silver, mirror-like flooring beneath us covered in fresh red and white rose petals. When we went up in the air and spun around, the fabric caught the petals and created a mini rose-petal tornado. We had no music, so all you could hear was our breath. It was truly exquisite and powerful, and it took me to a place I had never gone physically, emotionally, or spiritually. I knew from that moment on, this would be my "style" of aerial performance. I knew I would do more than just put on a show. I wanted to create works of art that spoke to the soul.

As beautiful as these performances are, they are also extremely taxing on the body. I've learned to live with permanent callusing on my wrists from all the one-armed flying I do. The fabric pulls very tightly and scrapes the skin off. After you do it over and over, your skin finally builds up a tolerance, but it looks ugly and is painful for a long time.

For a while, part of our act involved me picking up Nate while hanging upside down on the silks. He weighed 185 pounds, while I was around 95 pounds. It was excruciating at first, but once I lost weight, got in better shape, and built up the tolerance, it became second nature. Several aerialists I know have needed reconstructive shoulder surgery. When you're flying with one arm, you have to pull your shoulder blades in. Otherwise, you risk ripping or pulling your rotator cuff, causing serious and permanent damage. Thankfully, the worst I've ever had was a pull on my right shoulder, and I had to switch flying arms for about a month and a half. I always pull that shoulder blade in now. Lesson learned!

Yet even with all of these noteworthy experiences, booking gigs remained difficult. I wasn't your average aerialist or acrobat. In everyone's eyes, I was a risk, a liability. I was hearing all this chatter, and I had to keep focused and not blow my top every time someone turned us down. Nate did his best to shield me from it, but I knew what was holding us back. I'd tell bookers, "Just watch, just see what I can do. You'll get it." But we had a lot of people to convince. They worried I might slip and fall and hurt myself.

Of course, Nate was the one they usually voiced their concerns to. No one wanted to offend the girl without legs. I wish they would have just come out and said it: "You make us nervous." I don't get offended by this concern because I've had to deal with similar situations virtually every day of my life. I know what people think *might* happen. I know their hesitations, and they're wrong. What offends me is people *not* treating me like an adult and *not* being honest. What offends me is pity. But that's a battle I'll always have to fight.

All Eyes on Me

It wasn't until we booked Britney Spears's Circus Tour that things changed dramatically. It was the highest-grossing tour in the world in 2009. Without a doubt, God was making this happen for me! I didn't even audition. Nate and I were just hitting our stride as a team when he got the opportunity to join the tour. He felt quite guilty about being gone for so long when we had just gotten our act off the ground (literally!), but I insisted it was too good a gig for him to pass up. He started rehearsals and joined the tour in North America, all the while talking me up to his tour mates. When the show made a stop in Orlando, all the performers, dancers, specialty acts, and aerialists already knew who I was and wanted to meet me face-to-face, so I went backstage and visited with them.

The tour then went to Europe for a month or so before taking a break. I flew to Canada to greet Nate at the end of that tour leg and met the Circus gang again. This time we got a meeting with the three main men who ran the tour, and Nate and I showed them a video of our trampoline act. That's all it took. A few months later, I was officially on the Circus Tour as a featured performer. I did the entire second North American leg followed by the Australian tour. It was all a bit surreal. I had been in the entertainment industry for only a little over a year at this point (so green!), and I was performing in front of twenty thousand people a night. I gave myself a big pep talk: *Jen, you have two choices here. You either rise to the occasion or fail miserably with thousands of people watching.* When you don't have legs, you don't have the leeway to make any major mistakes. If I were to wipe out, it would have been a catastrophe and I would have kissed that job, not to mention my career, good-bye. Failure wasn't an option.

Before every show, I would find a dark corner, cover up my head with my black cloak, and spend a good twenty to thirty minutes praying and visualizing the entire act. Then it was time to go into the arena! The cloaks concealed our costumes so that no one knew we were performers as we walked through the audience. Then we would enter underneath the mammoth stage. Like a circus, it had three rings, the middle one being the biggest, with a huge LED screen projecting images of the show above it. All the action took place under the stage, and it bustled like a little city: the dancers stretched, the costume ladies pulled off lightning-quick changes, the hair and makeup artists applied last-minute touch-ups.

Britney always had an opening act. For a while it was Jordin Sparks, who was a super sweet girl. Later it was the Pussycat Dolls, who never failed to tear down the house. A twenty-minute break preceded the main concert, which started with a booming countdown: "10, 9, 8, 7, 6, 5, 4, 3, 2, 1 . . ." At this point, the audience went insane. When it was time for us to do our act, the "ceiling" would lower down, and we would step onto a platform. I would always rub Nate's head for good luck; that was my thing. All the guys had to shave their heads for the tour, so I liked that his was shiny and smooth. The platform would slowly raise us up into the audience until we were at the top of the stage. I remember seeing this vast sea of people screaming and the camera lights flashing. The air felt electric. The trampoline was already wheeled onto the stage at this point. This wasn't a run-of-the-mill, backyard trampoline—it was a twelve-by-fourteen-foot competitive trampoline with major bounce.

Then *bam!* The spotlight would hit us, and we'd enter from opposite sides of the middle ring, meeting in front of the trampoline. I was in my wheelchair, and Nate would go behind me, put his hands on my hips, and on the downbeat of the music hurl me backward, out of my chair and onto the trampoline. It was epic! No one expected it, and I'd always hear a huge gasp roll through the audience followed by a roar of cheers. My final pose was equally stunning: I'd bounce high in the air, do a half twist, and land on my back in Nate's arms high above him. The adrenaline rush was unreal.

It took me about ten shows to resolve my jittery nerves (I did about forty in total) so I could actually start to enjoy performing. One of the coolest moments on tour was when my parents, my close family friend Janice Henning, and my brother Brad came to see me. The closest stop to them was Chicago, so they all made a trip of it. I got them the "fifty-yard-line seats" smack-dab in the middle and up front so they'd have a great view. It was the first time they had ever seen me perform, and my mom said it took her breath away. I still tease my dad that he went to a Britney Spears concert (the music of Johnny Cash is so much more his speed!). In all the different cities we'd go to, we would get free tickets to give to friends and family. And after working at Disney, I had friends all over the country, so there was always someone I wanted to see. They'd come to the show and cheer me on.

I got to perform in Madison Square Garden three times (MTV News said our act was one of the top-five reasons to see the concert!), and in a huge arena in Australia, Britney actually stopped everything during a sound check to watch us rehearse. That night I remember being high up in Nate's arms on stage and thinking, *This is crazy! This is my life! God is so good!* Playing in concert arenas in front of twenty thousand people was thrilling, terrifying, and affirming all at once. It was my saving grace, and, Britney, I'll be forever grateful! As soon as we got back from touring, no one had to ask what people would think of me. No one worried that I couldn't cut it. The subject never came up, ever again. Performing on tour gave me confidence and credibility. I wasn't just a visitor to the entertainment world. I was here to stay.

In performing I found something that had been missing in my life: a sense of calmness and wholeness. Finding your own creative outlet is so important. It's not only a break and distraction from everyday life and stress, but it's also a time for you to connect with your inner self and channel your energy into something positive and productive. Tumbling gave me strength and confidence, while performing gave me peace and clarity. When I perform, I get swept away, lost, and no one and nothing exists but the moment. I put everything out on the table—all my emotions, my worries, my cares, my frustrations, my fears. Then I let them all fade away, and it heals my soul. It lights me up from every space of my innermost being. I swear, sometimes I feel like the light is literally bursting from every part of me and shining through. I've been all over the world (Dublin, Liverpool, Sydney, Dubai, Tokyo, Qatar, Düsseldorf, Amsterdam, Hong Kong, Malaysia, Chicago, Orlando, Boston, Austin, Los Angeles, and NYC to name a few), and with each show, I know with greater certainty that this is what I was born to do.

BELIEVE IT!

The Tiniest Deed
Can Make a Difference

How thankful am I that Nate saw potential in me and took me on to train, and that Britney and her team allowed me to perform on the Circus Tour? Very. I'm sure they didn't see it as a huge deal, but it completely changed my life. I realize now that sometimes things we don't see as "a biggie" are much more significant to others. Case in point: a young couple had a boy born without legs, just like me. His name is Brody. They didn't know what to do and were very worried and unsure about how to handle a child like this. They saw me on the news and somehow got in contact with my parents to ask their advice. Eventually, we all met up, and at just twelve years old, I proceeded to tell them how to coach their kid. "Don't set limits for him," I said, going on and on about how my parents had always let me try things, fail, and learn. They smiled, thanked me, and went back to their lives. I never thought much about it again. It was just a few minutes out of my life. But then I found out last year that Brody is now a young man and plays on the paralympic hockey team. Brody is now speaking publicly, motivating people, and he credits his success to me. *Me!* I had no idea how he was doing or how much of an impact I had on him and his family. I was completely baffled, humbled, and honored when I found this out. You never know when one small good deed can change someone's life for the better. So I say do them—each and every day.

CHAPTER NINE

This Heart of Mine

Love is patient, love is kind. It does not envy, it does not boast, it is not proud. It does not dishonor others, it is not self-seeking, it is not easily angered, it keeps no record of wrongs. Love does not delight in evil but rejoices with the truth. It always protects, always trusts, always hopes, always perseveres. Love never fails.

—1 Corinthians 13:4–8

I've always had an unusual heart—and not just because it's on the right side of my chest! I feel things intensely, and I love fiercely—much more than most people. For me, there is no wishy-washy "I love you, I love you not." When I love, it's with every fiber of my being. I'm in it 110 percent, and I don't know how to do it any other way. Sometimes this tsunami of emotions scares people off: it's too much, too deep, too fast. There was a time when I actually prayed to God to take away these feelings. Why? Because it hurt. It hurt to have someone not reciprocate. It hurt to love and then lose that love when the expectations I set were too high. For the longest time, I assumed everyone felt like I did. But I learned the hard way, that's not always the case.

I met my first real love, Dave, at Camp Illiana, the church camp I mentioned previously, when I was twelve. We barely spoke to each other that first summer, but he wrote me a letter shortly after. I couldn't remember exactly who he was (there were two Daves at camp), so I didn't respond. But for some reason, right before camp the next year, I remembered the letter, dug it out, and sent him an email. We agreed we'd meet up in line at registration. He told me he had blond hair and blue eyes, was about six feet tall, and would be wearing a baseball cap.

I remember waiting in line, glancing to my left, and noticing this cute guy walking by. I did a double take and realized he met the description perfectly. It was Dave! He recognized me and walked back to where I was sitting. The chemistry was instantaneous, and I think I stared a little too long. But I couldn't help it. He had the biggest smile, a goofy personality, and was an amazing athlete (the first in my pattern of dating athletes). He played basketball and tennis and ran cross-country. Also, like me, he was a hugger.

We spent that entire first week of camp together—every event, every meal. We sat next to each other in worship, and he was so much taller than I was, which I loved. But I always felt a little weird and embarrassed when everyone else stood up and I couldn't—it made the words on the screen hard to see. One day he noticed I was uncomfortable and did the sweetest thing: he stayed seated next to me. He never seemed to care what others thought—just that I was happy.

In only a couple of days, I was full-blown over the moon about him. I knew he was too shy to ever ask me out, so if I wanted things to go anywhere, I was going to have to put on my big-girl panties and just do it! I remember telling one of my friends in the dorm all about him, and she suggested I write him a letter, putting all my thoughts and feelings out there. His letter, after all, had started our whole attraction. What did I have to lose? So I wrote to him. I was 100 percent open and honest with exactly how I felt about him. I told him I loved spending time with him and confessed that my stomach got butterflies whenever he was around. Then I folded up the letter into a small square, wrote his name on top, and gave it to him that night before heading back to my cabin to sleep. This way, I reasoned, he'd have the night to read it, think about it, and then respond in the morning. I was anxious all night, tossing and turning. But I also knew no matter what his response was, not saying anything and always wondering "what if?" would have been worse.

I was up before everyone the next day and the first one in the shower room. I couldn't wait to get to the dining hall and find Dave. When I did, he had the biggest smile on his face, with those perfect teeth and adorable dimples. He said he couldn't believe how honest and bold I was. He never would have had the courage to tell me how he felt, which, it turned out, was exactly the same way I did.

Just like that, we became an item. Things could not have been more perfect. We were exactly six weeks apart in age (I was older), both just about to turn fourteen, and lived a little more than an hour away from each other. After camp ended, our parents would drive us to see each other every weekend. We met at an Amish barn called Dinky's Auction Center about fifteen minutes from Dave and about an hour from us. It had a huge wraparound porch with chairs and benches, and we could have a little alone time there. It's actually the place we shared our first kiss. We had been hanging out for a while, flirting and chatting, and he had his arm around me and was looking into my eyes.

"And this would be where you kiss me," I said, teasing him. When he did, it was like the Fourth of July at Disney World—insane fireworks. Our parents soon became good friends, and Janice, his mom, became best friends with my mom, so we'd often go on family trips together. For the longest time, it was "Jen & Dave," and we were so in love with everything about each other. For my fourteenth birthday, he bought me a gold ring with two diamonds. I was floored and never took it off. He was the first person I slow danced with at a school dance while wearing my prosthetics, looking deeply into his eyes. He told me if I would rather not wear them, he'd dance on his knees! At first I was mortified. "OMG, what are you doing?" But then I finally just caved in and let him do it.

Dave and I broke up the next year, and to say I was devastated would be a massive understatement. He was my first love, my first dating experience. He was the first boy I ever confessed my love to. It was the kind of love that is so pure and raw and exposed, the way you love before you've been hurt or jaded in other relationships. It was the kind of love where you hold nothing back and put every single ounce of your being into it. That was when I realized I didn't love like most people. I was so young, but I loved with such intensity and depth that when that love was gone, it took part of me with it. If you ask me why we broke up, I can't really put my finger on one reason. He was always more logical and analytical, the ying to my yang. He was a star athlete all through high school, received a full-ride academic scholarship to college, and landed a great job with the Ford Motor Company before he even graduated.

Although our romance faded, we maintained a very strong friendship for more than ten years. He was tough to get over. There will never be another Dave in my life, and I will always have a special place in my heart for him and will cherish all the memories we made together.

Taking Another Chance

I went out on a lot of dates after Dave and I broke up, but only two or three of those men would I have actually called my boyfriend. My last boyfriend was especially different

— *My VIPs* —

Family Friend (and Dave's Mom): Janice Henning

I have known Jen for coming up on fifteen years. Dave came home from church camp and said, "I met the coolest girl." At that age, Dave wasn't really into girls so much, so we were quite intrigued.

"Oh really?" his father and I said. "What is so cool about her?"

Imagine our surprise when he answered (with all seriousness), "She can beat me at arm wrestling." That was the start of several wonderful things. These two young teens who had a desire to spend time together brought their families together as well. Sharon, Jen's mom, and I grew to be best friends, and I got to know Jen and watch her grow into the beautiful young lady she is today.

Of course, I saw that coming: at thirteen, Jen seemed very confident and very outgoing. She had an "as-a-matter-of-fact" style about her. I did not have much experience dealing with a person with a handicap, and I did not get any experience from Jen because she never acted handicapped. To her, nothing is unattainable. She is thoughtful, intelligent, kind, inspiring, fun-loving, straightforward, humble, considerate, and someone I am delighted to call my friend.

I am thrilled that she has a special way of reaching people with her amazing story. She is gifted and joyful. To know her is to love her, and I do. To those of you reading this, if you have never had a Jen hug, you are missing out, because her hugs are as warm and delightful as her smile.

from the rest. We had a deep emotional connection, but our relationship ended abruptly. I was heartbroken on a new level. It felt as though someone had physically knocked the wind out of me. He was a solid artist and a solid Christian, and we connected on so many levels. After a year of being intensely in each other's lives, our relationship came crashing down, despite all my prayers to God that He "fix" it. So when it couldn't be fixed, who did I blame? Not myself, not my ex, but God. I remember saying for the first time, "I am so angry at You, God. Why would You allow this to happen to me?" I prayed for some explanation, but it didn't come. Most girls break up with a boyfriend and get over it. For me, there was no easy getting over it. Weeks and months passed before I finally realized something: God didn't owe me an explanation. Sometimes He's simply protecting us, and we have to trust that there is a lesson to be learned.

A year later, I finally had closure and could see the experience for what it truly was: a test of my faith. God wanted me to continue to grow in love—for Him and for others. I see it as a journey, the same way I view the rest of my life. Eventually, I will arrive at where I'm supposed to be. Eventually, I will find a man who is everything I'm looking for. I know I will, because I've come very close. My last boyfriend was such a beautiful Christian man. Six foot three, 230 pounds, strong and gentle at the same time. Not only was he respectful *and* romantic, but at Thanksgiving, he and my mom stood side by side as he helped her wash dishes. Ladies, guys like this *do* exist.

So yes, I'm an eternal optimist. I believe love exists for everyone if you're willing to put yourself out there. If you're willing to be open, honest, and vulnerable and to lay all the cards on the table, you'll find it. What is the alternative? To harden your heart and not let someone in? To never take the risk because you fear rejection? If something is worth having, then it's worth fighting for. I love in a way that I want to be loved. I love with faith that there is someone out there, ready and willing to welcome all I have to offer and also to return my love. I love knowing that when my heart feels broken and depleted, God will fill it up. He will lead me to opportunities and people that build me up again.

The word *love* can seem a little cliché. It's definitely overused and underrated. But don't doubt its power. I think Dr. Martin Luther King Jr. said it best: "Hate cannot drive out hate; only love can do that." I love (pun intended) that quote because, to me, love can tear down all boundaries, all enemies, all walls. It can heal a heart that refuses to be open to anyone or anything. It's very easy to love someone when they love you back. But the real test of character comes from loving someone who seems "unlovable," showing them kindness when they're not capable of doing the same because they're hurt, insecure, or afraid. When you respond to that person with support and compassion, you are allowing them to feel what it's like to be accepted, respected, embraced. You change lives. You bring someone closer to God because He *is* love.

Where Love Began

I think my philosophy about love comes from a variety of places. My parents taught me what love is, not just through their words but through their actions. Nothing I could have done or said would have made them stop loving me. They might have been disappointed and had to discipline me, but I knew at the end of the day that their love was unwavering.

For a kid who fought back tears at all costs, I was actually extremely sensitive and empathetic. I could never watch *Bambi*, *The Fox and the Hound*, or *All Dogs Go to Heaven* because the animals dying in those animated movies was just too overwhelmingly sad for me to handle.

"Jennifer, it's a cartoon," my brothers would tease me. But it didn't matter. I would mentally put myself right in Bambi's place and could not (still cannot) bear to see his mama die in the woods. Just thinking about it, I get all choked up!

My dad liked to watch the Discovery Channel's wildlife stories—the ones where the animals hunt and kill each other, survival of the fittest. While my brothers gathered around the TV, mesmerized, I couldn't be in the same room.

My parents were empathetic as well, but more so regarding people as opposed to mountain lions and animated deer. I remember once when a story came on the news about a family losing their home in a fire on Christmas. My family and I were all watching together, and a sad silence fell over our living room before my mom let out an anguished sigh. Our hearts went out to them, and we felt their pain in such a powerful, palpable way.

So in the Bricker house, my heart was encouraged to grow and grow. Animals weren't the only objects of my affection. There was Mikey, my large baby troll with vibrant blue hair and a jewel in his belly button. Mikey had a whole wardrobe of clothes that I kept clean and unwrinkled. I combed his hair so it was out of his eyes. I carried him with me everywhere (otherwise he'd be lonely) and insisted he sit at the dinner table and be part of the family discussion. My parents didn't discourage me—they thought it was wonderful that I could care so much. They were thrilled that I naturally had compassion for the world around me and all who inhabit it.

To this day, my friends will tease me. "Jen, you're all about strength, but you're really such a softie." I am, and I'm proud of that fact. Sometimes I can feel another person's pain as clearly as if it were my own. It's something I remind myself to be conscious of. My dad would call it "taking a walk in someone's shoes." We're so busy in our daily lives, caught up in our to-do lists and personal agendas, that it's easy to become jaded, self-absorbed, or uncaring. But compassion is something to practice every day. It moves mountains. It erases anger, resentment, and prejudice, and it brings peace and forgiveness. It plants the seeds of change. It's right there in the Bible in Galatians 6:2, which reads, "Carry each other's burdens, and in this way you will fulfill the law of Christ." Acknowledging a person's feelings is one of the most beautiful things you can do for another soul. Truly, it's simple to say, "I hear you. I see what you're going through. I'm sorry." The first step in healing someone's pain and suffering is being present. Some people think showing sympathy makes you weaker, but the opposite is true. It makes you stronger and wiser, and allows you to fully realize the deep connection that exists between all people, regardless of who they are or where they come from.

Be Grateful

Gratitude is another way to show love. I'm not suggesting you go out and buy flowers and candy for everyone who's ever been nice to you. Simply tell them, "I appreciate that you're in my life." Case in point: my friend Courtney Grant. That's his name, but my family and I call him Grant. Grant came into my life in 2008, while I was living in Orlando. My roommate and I needed a third roommate in our apartment, and he was it. We instantly clicked. I was twenty and he was nineteen. We were both just starting our careers—he was modeling and I was performing. Just two young, broke "kids" trying to live our dreams. I knew I could always count on him. He's a hard worker and a survivor, and God put us together for many reasons. I was able to give him the love he never had growing up, and he in return gave me a solid, lasting friendship.

I remember our first Thanksgiving together—we knew with our limited income it would be sparse. I never liked to tell my parents when I needed money because I didn't want to burden or worry them. But Grant knew I'd be bummed if we didn't do something traditional.

I came home that Thanksgiving evening after work to find a note on the door. It read:

Turkey—$15
Sweet potatoes—$5
Cranberries—$3
Pumpkin pie—$6

The look on your face when you open the door—Priceless!

I opened the door to find that Grant had moved our kitchen table into the middle of the living room. The lights were dim, candles were lit, and there was an entire Thanksgiving feast laid out just for us. I will never in my life forget that moment, and I will never forget that it came on Thanksgiving, a time when we show our gratitude and give thanks. It couldn't have been more perfect.

Grant moved to LA a year after I did to pursue his modeling/acting career. I already had an apartment for us, ready and waiting. Since we first met, we've been penniless, lived together in two different states, and wanted to strangle each other on more than one occasion. We've laughed, we've cried, we've been through serious highs and lows with our bodies, our careers, our relationships. I know at the end of the day, if anything were to go wrong for me, Grant would be there in a heartbeat.

This book lets me show my gratitude to so many people who have been there for me in a big, 200-plus-page kind of way. But it doesn't have to be that wordy! A simple thank-you will suffice. Count your blessings—that's gratitude to God. I find that when I do, my perspective shifts from me, me, me and what I'm lacking to all the abundance He's already shown me. When you're ambitious (guilty as charged!), it's a tricky road to walk. You want things, you desire things, you are driven to achieve things. Ambition is good—it fuels your passion and your purpose. But it's not everything. It's important to take stock of all the good in your life right here, right now. You can do it in a journal or in a prayer. You can do it in a simple phone call or by sending an email or text. When you do, there's an instant lift in your life and your way of thinking. You'll feel happier, healthier, and more optimistic when you take the time to be grateful.

God Heals the Heart

Romantic love is not for the weak of heart. It's not a matter of *if* you get hurt but a matter of *when*. Scientists actually say the pain we experience emotionally when a heart breaks is as strong as physical pain. So why do we put ourselves through it? Because we're human. Because we crave someone to come home to, to confide in, to nurture, to wake up with, and to share our deepest secrets and dreams with. Because in every loss, there is also a gain. People often tell me they've given up on love, and I remind them that God makes beauty out of ashes. It's what He's in the business of doing. I believe that true, pure love is attainable. I believe someone is out there who will be loyal and dependable, and who will fight for me. He will be my warrior and my rock, my lover and my best friend. Maybe I'm naive, but I think love is magical. It's one of the most powerful things you can experience here on this earth. The more we understand God and His love, the deeper we can love others. I don't think humans ever reach a "love limit." You have to hold out for the person you are head over heels for, all cylinders firing. You have to have faith that it is not only possible, but it's also what God wants for you.

I have tried several times in my life to reopen doors that God has closed. I can almost hear Him telling me, "Jen, this guy is not meant for you. Stop trying to get him back." It's an unhealthy cycle, I know. But I've had to go through it to realize that God knows the beginning, the middle, and the end—even if I don't. He loves me through all things, including my failures, my faults, and my heartbreaks. Psalm 147:3 tells us, "[God] heals the brokenhearted and binds up their wounds." And David knew that "the LORD is close to the brokenhearted and saves those who are crushed in spirit" (Ps. 34:18). God wants us to take comfort in knowing that heartache is temporary—He's on it! What He has in store for us is much better than we could ever imagine.

Heartbreak is different for everyone who experiences it. Sometimes it's in the moment—as in my awful breakup. Sometimes it's the weight of the past and a near lifetime of regret. My birth mother, Camelia, has had an extremely difficult time letting go of the heartbreak of giving me up for adoption. That loss consumed her for so long that it was difficult for her to see or speak to me without blaming herself and reliving that dark, painful period in her life. But like me, she's a woman of great faith. Slowly, her heart is healing. We have a long way to go in our relationship, but God is working to make her whole again, to help her regain what she thought was lost forever. That's the other great thing about real, true love: it never dies.

Love Yourself First

You can have a happy relationship—either friendship or romance—only if you love yourself first. When you don't love yourself, what ends up happening is that you put all your expectations for happiness on another human being instead of on God—and that's a recipe for disaster. Human beings are fragile and flawed. We disappoint and make mistakes. And how can you expect someone to love you for who you are if you don't love and know yourself? How can you expect to be adored and appreciated when you look in the mirror and hate what you see? Again, it's a simple equation: what you put out there equals what you get back. Love yourself and you will be lovable.

Of course, that's easier said than done. I've had a lot of body issues to contend with. As a kid I hated my big, bulky arms, but things really escalated when I was twenty years old and twenty pounds heavier than I am now. I think the weight gain was due to the stress of being on my own, coupled with the fact that I had no idea how to eat healthy. My four basic food groups were Pasta Alfredo, pizza, pop, and fast food. Growing up, it didn't seem much of an issue to be chubby. To be honest, most people where I'm from were at least a few pounds overweight. We eat fried food and corn bread, and we're okay with it! But once I entered the entertainment world, I realized my body type was far from ideal. Everyone looked like chiseled Greek statues to me: rock-hard abs, sculpted arms and shoulders, buns you could bounce a quarter off of!

When I started training with Nate, we would meet up five days a week and train for two to three hours. I started reading health and nutrition books, trying to figure out how to think of food as fuel—not just something to fill my face with. One morning I woke up and noticed all my clothes were too big on me. I had lost fifteen pounds, but that was just the start.

In 2011, when I was living in LA, I had my first workout with my trainer, Eric Fleishman ("Eric the Trainer"). His specialty is body transformation, but in my case, it was a mental as well as physical change. He showed me what to eat and what not to eat: bye-bye pasta, rice, potatoes, and my favorite whole-wheat bagels topped with peanut butter and bananas! My first meal of the day became an egg-white omelet with half a can of tuna and half a cup of chopped veggies, topped with a spoonful of avocado and salsa. Most of the exercises we did were for the lower body—ironic for a girl with no legs! We did crunches, kick-ups, hydrants, and endless push-ups. I was worried it would make my arms bigger—always my pet peeve. But Eric promised it wouldn't,

— *My VIPs* —

Best Trainer Ever: Eric Fleishman

You know that magical, positive energy that makes any normal situation special? It's the difference between a regular action film and a James Bond movie. That's the sparkle that Jen Bricker possesses. And her positive vibe is contagious! Jen can cheer up any grumpy person. Essentially, she turns any ordinary day into a James Bond movie.

---

and he was right. By age twenty-four, I'd lost thirty pounds, nearly five inches from my waist, and six inches off my hips. I was the leanest I'd ever been and living strong in a body I had thought would never be possible for me.

Soon after, enamored with my new body, I became obsessed with being and staying thin. When size 00 shorts were hanging off me, I wasn't satisfied. I felt myself being dragged into a dangerous and dark downward spiral. I had body dysmorphic disorder (BDD), though I couldn't admit it at the time. It's self-loathing: your head just gets stuck on these negative thoughts about how you look and keeps playing them back to you like a scratched vinyl record. No matter how many people told me I looked great/fine/beautiful, I didn't believe it and couldn't see it. I would stare at myself in the full-length mirror in my bedroom, scrutinizing every angle, standing sideways, checking out my butt, pinching every inch of flesh. With each glance, I would tear myself apart. I was relentless and merciless: *What's that poof in my stomach? Does my face look rounder? Do I look fat?* I started eating so little that my hair was thinning, my periods became irregular, and I was miserable. I didn't go to parties or meet people in restaurants because I didn't want to be tempted by food. Instead, I would meet them in a coffee shop so I could order just a cup of tea.

My friend Grant finally sat me down and gave me a stern talking to. "Jen, you're too skinny," he said. "You've lost your butt; you've lost your boobs. Your eyes are all sunken in! What are you doing to yourself? You have to stop!"

I was so defensive and angry. "Are you kidding me? Do you know how hard I've worked to look like this?" I didn't talk to him for a few days until I realized he was 100 percent right. I wasn't healthy. And worse than that, this false body image I'd created for myself—this impossible ideal—was stealing my light and my joy. I hadn't been fully Jen for a long time, and I didn't know how to get her back. I think that whole experience brought me much closer to God because I was so far down that I didn't know how I would get up. I had to pray constantly and ask Him to help me find my way back.

I began with affirmations. I told myself, "You are *not* fat. You are beautiful in God's eyes." I let those words sink in. Finally, I challenged myself to go forty days without looking at my body in a mirror. I covered the full-length mirror in my bedroom with photos of things that made me happy: pictures of me doing gymnastics and of friends and family and home, articles about me in magazines. Suddenly that mirror stopped pointing a finger and instead became a symbol of all of God's gifts. That giant collage brought me back to liking and loving myself and being grateful for the body I'm in. I'm still not going to let much junk food cross these lips, and I'm still going to work out hard—but I'm going to love what God created and not punish myself for failing to fit into a certain mold. I'd spent so much of my life trying to bust out of stereotypes, and here I was thinking I had to look and be a certain way.

I'm probably never going to look like anyone else, and that's fine. I kind of like to stand out in a crowd.

BELIEVE IT!

Mr. Right Is Out There

I've made enough mistakes in my dating life to know now the things that do and don't work for me. The perfect man for me is someone who is trustworthy, honest, sincere, and polite, and who calls instead of texts. He has a sense of humor and a sense of adventure. He doesn't play mind games and respects my mind. He's out there. I've always said I'll be single for the rest of my life before I settle, but I know I won't have to. My parents have given me one strong bit of advice on the subject (since then they've butted out): make sure the person you choose is someone you can sit and talk with, because when you're retired, that's what you do all day! They should know; they've been married forty-three years. Love can't just be about that instant attraction (although that's part of it). It has to be deeper. There needs to be not only chemistry but also a connection. I do believe in soul mates, and I have faith that God has one for me.

CHAPTER TEN

Ordinary Heroes

It is not by sword or spear that the LORD saves; for the battle is the LORD's.

—1 Samuel 17:47

My favorite Bible story is David and Goliath, probably because it's about the little guy (I can totally relate) who goes up against the giant and defeats him. I can't imagine how terrifying it must have been for David to face Goliath—an enormous, trained, and skilled soldier. David had none of Goliath's skills or size, and if anyone was betting, I guarantee no one was putting any money on him.

So what made David so heroic? What gave him the courage to go up against the toughest odds and the fiercest opponent? Faith. He knew he was called by God to defeat the great warrior, and he fought boldly in faith. I love this story because it relates so much to real life. We all have "Goliaths" in our lives. They may not be giant warriors. Maybe they're not even people but are, instead, situations or circumstances. Whenever I find myself fighting against the odds, whenever I feel overwhelmed and outmatched, I turn to God to inspire me. Through Him, everything is possible. Didn't He prove that with David?

This story also reminds me that anyone can be a hero. You don't have to be born into it. You don't have to have status or money or a fancy education. Everyone has their own definition of what it means to be a hero. I love Marvel Comics superheroes, but the tights and cape aren't necessary to exhibit heroic qualities. In my mind, heroes are people I admire, look up to, respect, revere. People who, in the moment, do something selfless and noble, generous and genuine. They go out of their way to make a difference in someone's life or the world as a whole, with little fear of what others might think or say.

As I'm writing this, I'm thinking to myself, *This description fits my parents to a T*. Yet neither of them would *ever* admit that. That's another heroic quality: humility. My mom will tell you that I blessed her life more than she ever blessed mine. And my dad? He would shrug it off as "no big deal." It was a big deal to me! When I think of how much my parents did to ensure I was happy, healthy, confident, and safe, I wonder, *How can I fill those shoes?* I don't know, but I'll try. I'll try to live up to their examples when I'm a parent to my own kids.

My family is filled with heroes. When my brother Brian joined the navy, it certainly made him a hero in my eyes. I was about ten years old when we visited him on his ship when he was stationed in Virginia. For the record, since I was very young, I have always insisted on calling Brian "Bubba" and got flat-out offended when anyone else did the same. It was my nickname for him, no one else's! Bubba would fight for me without me needing to ask—he has in the past. One time our whole family was shopping in a Sam's Club, and some guy came over to us and made a nasty comment about "bringing a cripple out in public." Bubba jumped at him, saying a few choice words, and my parents had to talk Bubba down.

My friend Grant would also fight for me. After I first moved to LA, I had a really tough time getting a job. I know! Me of all people! I love talking to people and am a highly efficient worker, so why on earth couldn't I find a job for nine months? While I was living in Florida, I had no trouble at all. But in LA, I started to see a pattern evolving. I would interview, things would go well, and then nothing. They'd pass me over for someone else.

I asked Grant if he thought it was because people were afraid to hire someone in a wheelchair. Neither of us could believe that was the issue—it was such out-and-out discrimination. Then one day I called a store that was hiring, and the man on the phone told me to come right in. "You sound like the perfect candidate!" he told me enthusiastically.

When I got there, he took one look at me and paused. I know that pause. I know that look. Then he stammered, "Uh, let me go get a paper in the back." I said okay, and then I waited . . . and waited . . . and waited. I looked around, and all the other employees were looking at me. One of them shook her head and said, "I'm so sorry." I realized what was happening: he wasn't coming back. He wasn't even going to give me the opportunity to apply.

I think I literally had steam coming out of my ears. I flew out of the store in total shock. I had never been treated like that before. Grant had been waiting outside the store for me, and when I told him what had happened, he instantly got that look on his face.

"Wait!" I said, grabbing his arm. "Stop! Don't do it!"

But it was too late—there was no holding him back. "I'm going in there," he said. "You can either stay out here or come in with me." Of course I went back in. I was afraid of what he might do, and the last thing I wanted was a big scene. Grant asked for the clerk, and he finally came out of hiding. They got into a huge argument in the middle of the

— *My VIPs* —

My Friend: Cody Craig

It was the summer of 2003. I saw a really cute girl with no legs at the county fair (ugh, that sounds so hillbilly). I decided to say hello, not realizing what an amazing person she would become and already was. We discovered that we had friends in common and soon became friends ourselves. Three years later, I took Jen to her senior prom. It was the only time I ever saw her wear artificial legs. Her dad showed me how to release the knee joint so that she could sit in my car. To do so, he had to reach under her dress. Despite the knee joint being nowhere near actual flesh, he said, "I'm going to allow you to reach up here" in complete seriousness as he showed me how to release the joint.

In the winter of 2012, I saw Jen's Facebook post saying she was looking for a roommate and decided to pack up and move to California. I had the most wonderful experi-

store, and I was between the both of them, trying to referee. I couldn't believe the clerk was arguing instead of apologizing! Amazingly, the other employees saw what was going on and spoke up in my defense. They weren't on his side.

Well, a month or so later, Grant actually got hired at the store (go figure) and learned that the clerk had been fired after the incident! I just hope he took away something positive and learned a lesson from the experience. And I hope he reacts differently the next time. I've learned as I've gotten older to keep my temper in check. I never want to be the one

ence living with her. She loves Pop-Tarts, but they're not part of her healthy lifestyle, so I had to give her a piece of mine every time I ate one when she was around. She made it so much easier to meet new people because she was always meeting new people herself. She once arrived at a church community group by herself and, when confronted with a set of stairs, climbed the stairs while dragging her wheelchair behind her. She wears a ridiculous old-lady hat when going for walks in the park but still manages to look cute.

She is a terrible backseat driver, although, oddly enough, this didn't come up once when we drove halfway across the country together and had such great conversation that we never turned on the radio. She puts on an eye mask when she sleeps and lies flat on her back like a vampire. She would almost always get up before me in the morning and get my iPad from behind my air mattress to watch TV or browse the internet. Although she tried to be quiet, she woke me up almost every time.

Jen is one of the people I admire most in the world.

pitching a fit or causing a scene. I feel that only feeds and fuels the stereotype that disabled people are too politically correct and difficult and sensitive. I know better ways to get a point across. But I have to admit, having Grant there to defend and stand up for me that day was kind of nice. I never have to worry—my friends have my back.

Not all heroes are strong defenders. Some are quiet, hidden champions we never know about or even notice. They are humbly and secretly awesome, and never brag about it. They don't need to advertise it on a billboard or broadcast it over the internet. Many people give their time, money, and love to the less fortunate and ask for nothing in return—not even an acknowledgment. Those kind of people are my heroes—they are game changers and life changers. Others are heroes because they live their lives authentically—what you see is what you get. They will never change or hide who they are or what they believe to be popular or to meet the status quo. They speak their truths and inspire others to do the same.

I was introduced to Francis Chan's writing in the beginning of 2010 when I first started going to Real Life church in Orlando. My community group read his book *Crazy Love* together. Francis is an amazing giver. He's a pastor, a bestselling author, and the founder and chancellor of Eternity Bible College. He gives away about 90 percent of his income, doesn't take a salary from his church, and has donated most of his book royalties to charities. Each week my group went through a different chapter, reflected on it, and discussed its relevance to our own lives. Then we watched Francis's videos to take the study even deeper. That book opened my eyes to the concept of truly practicing what you preach. Francis is a hero to me because he leads a truly authentic life. He is on fire for God, and his passion helped ignite my own faith. His honesty and rawness are absolutely heroic to me, and he's someone I've always wanted to meet in person. I would be blown away.

Another personal hero of mine is Nick Vujicic. He's an Australian-born motivational speaker who was born with Phocomelia, a rare disorder that caused him to be born missing all four limbs. He grew up struggling, yet God helped him overcome many physical and emotional obstacles. God clearly wanted me and Nick to meet. In September 2014, I got a last-minute call to be a part of a red-carpet charity event in Dallas, Texas. The same night I flew in, the organizers of the event invited twenty or so of the participants to a big dinner in the hotel. I remember there was a very long table, and I slid all the way down to the middle so everyone else could pile in. A guy slid in next to me and introduced himself as Raymund King, Nick's lawyer.

We started chatting, and he said, "This was totally meant to happen. This is a 'God thing.' You and Nick have got to meet." I didn't really know much about Nick, but I knew of him. Thanks to Raymund, a few weeks later Nick invited me to be his guest at a speech he was giving at the Beverly Hilton Hotel. When I entered the hotel, he was seated on the lobby couch, just chilling before this enormous event. I envy his coolness!

From the minute I met Nick, he was gracious, kind, warm, and an all-around awesome guy. Communication was very natural between us. We get each other on so many levels. Then he went into this huge conference space and introduced me to the crowd. I couldn't believe it. I was so humbled and honored that he would take the time out of his speech to mention me! This was his day, his moment, and he wanted to share it. But that's how Nick is—selflessly kind and generous with his life, his time, and his wisdom. We've since developed a great friendship, and he was even gracious enough to write the foreword for this book. He's fully given his life to God for the true good of others. He's a remarkable human being whom I am now proud to call a friend.

The Hero Inside

Sometimes you have to be your own hero. What I mean by this is that you have to fight for what you believe in and for what you want to happen. Don't wait for a knight in shining armor to charge in and do it for you.

Maya Angelou, another one of my personal heroes, said, "Success is liking yourself, liking what you do, and liking *how* you do it." If you don't like something in your life, then change it. If something is holding you back, then conquer it. If you're unhappy, then do something to regain your joy. Trust me on this: Superman and Spidey may be otherwise occupied. Understand that your life is your own. It's God's gift to you. Be responsible for your choices, good and bad. It's truly in your hands. You choose your behavior, and you choose how to handle the consequences. If you're stuck, then get yourself unstuck. And before you use the word *can't*, remember how I feel about that! You can and you should, and you owe it to yourself to live the happiest, fullest life possible. Is it easier to rely on others, to blame or hold them responsible for what's wrong or missing in your life? Sure. Is it easier to make excuses and complain? Absolutely. But all of those things are cop-outs. You are responsible for what you do with your life. Will you be the person God wants you to be or a lesser version of yourself?

BELIEVE IT!

Everyone Is Equal in God's Eyes

Before I moved to LA, I had never seen a homeless person before. I would pass by them on the street, never offering food or money, and often looking away. I assumed (as a lot of people do) that they were drug addicts or alcoholics and not worthy of my time or concern. Since then, I've had the privilege of volunteering on Skid Row, the most dangerous street in LA. I've served the homeless food and learned their names and their personal backgrounds and stories. What I know now is that everyone is a few bad decisions away from being homeless—it could be you; it could be me. When I see someone on the street, I not only offer them money but also treat them as a person. I remind myself not to judge too quickly or too harshly. What they do is between them and God, and how I act and react is between me and God. Remember that everyone is fighting a battle, whether or not it is visible to others. Be kind, be generous, be humble. Everyone is equal in God's eyes and equally deserving of love and respect.

CHAPTER ELEVEN

Endless Possibilities

I will instruct you and teach you in the way you should go; I will counsel you with my loving eye on you.

—Psalm 32:8

ll of my little escapades and each and every one of my triumphs have been the result of me pushing myself. If something makes me uncomfortable, that's my signal that I need to do it. Comfortable is easy, comfortable is safe. But if I went through life simply content to be comfortable, I never would have found performing. I never would have seen the world. I never would have gotten so close to God. My life would be drab and colorless. I also never would have tried scuba diving!

Obviously, scuba is a lot easier if you have legs. And there's a bit of training involved to prepare for diving. First, you have to sit at the bottom of a pool and complete a series of "exercises." Sitting eight feet deep in a pool isn't so bad when you know that if you panic you can always pop right up to the surface. But when you get more advanced, you have to sit on the ocean floor (a lot deeper!), and you can't just shoot up to the surface (unless you want to bust an eardrum). Thinking about doing this didn't bother me much. I'm strong, and I figured that even without legs I could easily paddle myself back up to the surface.

But then came the time to actually do the exercises. I was okay taking my regulator (the thing that gives you oxygen) out of my mouth. I was fine swimming with the huge tanks that are bigger than I am and being deep, deep down below the surface of the water. But what totally got me, what made me cringe and set my heart racing with panic, was having to let my mask fill up with water. I wanted so badly to breathe through my nose, but when water has filled your mask, you can't.

When I first tried this at the bottom of a pool, it caught me off guard because it felt like I was choking. I freaked and shot straight up above the water to catch my breath. But as I advanced in my training, I had to do this same exercise at the bottom of the ocean. Like I said, when you're thirty feet down, you can't simply scramble to the top of the water to catch your breath. So I knew I had no option but to override my fear. My internal pep talk went something like this: *Jen, you're fine. The water hitting your nose sucks, so just don't breathe in with your nose. Keep focused on breathing in and out, in and out with your mouth and your regulator. You know this skill; you've done it before; it's fine. You're safe, and the only way you're not going to be safe is if you freak out.*

I let the water rush into my mask, and as my brain was trying to talk the rest of my body out of panicking, I just sat there for a while *being*. Instead of fighting my fear, I gave in to it. I let it exist beside me until it no longer scared me.

This is how I handle most things that frighten me in life: I sit with them and make peace. For me, the much scarier thing is to be complacent. If you become too used to everything and nothing ever changes, how will you ever grow or evolve? I was comfortable in Orlando. When Nate suggested we move to LA, that water-in-the-mask feeling grabbed me. I didn't know many people there and didn't even have a church to go to, not to mention I wasn't sure I could ever make a decent living with our act. But when God wants something for you, He'll make it happen. Off I went.

For me, taking on a new challenge means putting my faith in God in a big way. Most of the time I feel like I'm a spectator of my own life, watching this crazy show play out. Or I'm gripping, white-knuckled, onto the front seat of a roller coaster, and I don't know when it might speed up, go backward, corkscrew, or come to a screeching halt. That's where faith comes in. Sometimes it's absolutely terrifying. But God has never let me down, and He isn't going to start anytime soon.

I have a mammoth wish list of things I want to do, places I want to see, tasks I want to accomplish—and I'm always adding to it. I never want to be "done." I never want to get to a place where I'm stagnant or bored or stuck. I think every day is an opportunity to learn something new and move forward—even just an inch will do. Right now I'm determined to become fluent in Spanish. I have a *huge* passion and desire for all things Spanish. I like exercising my brain as much as I like exercising my body. Stop doing either and you lose your edge.

Writing this book was a huge new challenge for me. I had no idea where or how to begin, or the places it would lead me to. I prayed every time before I wrote, asking God for the words. I trusted that God would do most of the authoring, and He did. I feel His presence in every word. I suspected I'd learn a lot about writing and publishing but had no idea I'd learn so much about myself in the process. What people don't tell you about writing is that it's a little like therapy. You have to dig deep and be 100 percent honest, not just with your readers, but with yourself. But now that I've done it, I want to do more. I feel like I have dozens more stories to tell, things happening to me and impacting me every day. When people ask me what I do, I have a long-winded answer: athlete, performer, writer, speaker. I hope to add skydiver to that résumé any day now, and only God knows what else!

The Choice Is Yours

We all have decisions to make every day. For example, will you choose to be happy (because I do think happiness is a choice) or sad? Will you choose to focus on the can't or the can? Will you choose to be optimistic or pessimistic? Encouraging or discouraging? And the list goes on and on. What I've learned so far in my short time on earth is that the little choices we make—the small, the mundane, the minuscule ones—make the big ones possible. I don't always wake up on the right side of the bed, and I don't automatically ooze inspiration. I start every morning by reading the Bible and praying to get my mind and perspective straight and to ready myself for a day filled with choices. As my day progresses, am I going to let my circumstances get the best of me? Will I become a victim of my situation or my fears and anxieties? Or will I pray about them, give them to God, and let them go? First Peter 5:7 says, "Cast all your anxiety on him because he cares for you." One of the greatest gifts God gives us is free will—the ability to make our own decisions. But remember that He is all-knowing and all-seeing. When you make a choice, you have to live with it. Or, as my mom might say, "You made your bed. Now you have to lie in it." Keeping this in mind makes figuring out the right choices so much easier for me. What would God want, expect, appreciate? He never forces us to love, obey, or respect Him. Again, that's a choice.

I talk a lot about what's possible, and I have a very simple answer for you: anything you think, feel, dream, or imagine. Why not? What's standing in your way? If something is possible, then all it needs is a plan. If you have to get a little creative, then go for it. I put roller skates on my hands! I

– *My VIPs* –

My Dad: Gerald Bricker

I remember Jen was a little bitty thing, and we were on a sandbar fishing. I turned around to see her wiggling and wiggling her little butt deep into the sand, burying herself in it. What was she up to? It took me a moment to realize she had hooked into a big fish and had reared back and was trying to reel it in. So I started laughing, and she got all mad at me. "What is so funny?" she demanded. I said, "Nothing," and just watched her bring it on in. She didn't need my help. Never did. Nothing was too fast or too big or too hard for her. I had a three-wheeler, and it was a fast one, and she would go mudding on it with friends. All I had to do was put a hand control on, and she took off like lightning. She would snowboard in the winter, just grabbing on with two hands and throwing herself forward down the hill. The only thing she struggled with—of all things—was reaching the light switches in our house. She'd be grabbing all kinds of stuff and stretching up high to reach them. So I rigged up sticks from old venetian blinds so she could just push or pull on them to turn on the lights. We were always telling her, "You can do anything you want to do." We just had to figure it out and off she'd go.

think possibilities should be as wide as the sky and as vast as the ocean. In my case, some are silly and frivolous (a girl can dream, can't she?), while others are more serious and meaningful. But the point is that this list will continue to grow, and I'll never stop adding to it.

My Wish List . . . Right Now

- ☐ I want a house with a trampoline and high ceilings for my aerial rigging so I can perform and train at home. I'd like this space to be a full aerial/acrobatic gym so other performers can also have a free, creative, and artistic place to train.
- ☐ I would love to create a performing arts scholarship program in my hometown and provide a health and nutrition program for the community as well.
- ☐ I want a movie screen in my backyard with a fire pit, couches, and pillows so my guests and I can lounge and enjoy an outdoor movie. White twinkling lights would be strung in the trees to give it a magical feel. And I definitely need a hot tub and several hammocks. Just sayin' . . .
- ☐ I'd like to perform with Carrie Underwood, Josh Groban, or Céline Dion—they would sing and I'd do an interpretive aerial routine. How powerful would that be? I'd also love to play the opening ceremony of the Olympics or the halftime show at the Super Bowl. The bigger the audience, the better.
- ☐ I would like to have my own talk show and/or cohost a show or star in a sitcom dramedy where I play myself, kinda like *Seinfeld*! I think inspiring through art is one of the best ways to influence people, and you get to have fun while you're at it.
- ☐ I want to eat and perform my way through Italy and sail the Greek isles!
- ☐ Once in my life, I want to take off for a month and roam Europe, soaking up the culture, sampling the cuisine, and visiting friends. I'd love to take one vacation with everyone—brothers, sisters, and Mom and Dad.
- ☐ I want to perform with an orchestra and also at a huge Christian concert/event/gathering like Catalyst or the Harvest Crusades or Saddleback (Rick Warren's church) or a Hillsong concert.

- ☐ I want to perform on my fabric while Adele sings.
- ☐ I want to wow the president and first lady at the White House and perform on Jimmy Fallon's late-night talk show with my parents watching in the audience (they're huge fans).
- ☐ I'm looking forward to one day seeing a movie made about my life. I know God plans to touch many, many lives with the story He's given me to share.
- ☐ I want to be in one of Tyler Perry's movies.
- ☐ I would like to meet Garth Brooks, Oprah, Eva Mendes, George Foreman, and Steven Seagal, and have a nice long chat with each of them over a cup of tea! George and Steve: I'm also down for an arm wrestle!
- ☐ I want to be a hot wife, mom, and grandma. I want my health and nutrition to always be a priority. I want to always stay in rockin' shape for myself and for my husband to keep the fire burning well into my golden years!
- ☐ I want to be on the cover of *Shape, Fit,* or *Women's Health,* and have an artsy, beautiful spread in *Vogue, Glamour,* or *Vanity Fair.* Or maybe I'll be the next CoverGirl. I want to change the way people think about beauty.
- ☐ I want to team up with Under Armour (campaign, billboards, commercials) and break the internet with a positive message/image that inspires the world.
- ☐ I want to speak from my heart to as many millions of people as possible. I want to be a catalyst for clean, purposeful living and thinking outside of the box.
- ☐ I want to write a children's book (*Super Jen!*) and inspire kids to love reading, just as I did when I was younger.
- ☐ Most important, I want my relationship with God to grow stronger, deeper, and more meaningful every day. I want my faith to be unshakable and my gratitude for all His blessings to be unending!

BELIEVE IT!

You Create Your Own Peace of Mind

Clearly, I'm hard to slow down. As a result, I have a tough time relaxing, shutting off my brain, and just letting go. The one place I seem to be able to make that happen is up in the air. Whether I'm performing my aerial act or flying in a plane, something about being airborne grounds me. It's an odd juxtaposition! I've also learned to summon my senses. By this, I mean notice how things smell, sound, feel, taste. Try it. Breathe slowly and actually register what your body is doing. You don't always have to be on autopilot. Instead, feel your heart beat and the air come in and out of your lungs. Be present in the moment and allow yourself to truly experience where you are and what you're doing. It sounds so obvious, but so few of us actually do this throughout the course of our days. I know when I do, it's amazing what comes to mind. I do my best thinking in these quiet moments of clarity.

CHAPTER TWELVE

The Me Nobody Knows

Questions, Answers, and Tidbits

Commit your way to the LORD; trust in him and he will do this: He will make your righteous reward shine like the dawn, your vindication like the noon-day sun.

—Psalm 37:5–6

I said when I started writing this book that I would be totally, 100 percent honest—and I mean what I say. Not even my closest of friends and family completely know all the sides of me. They couldn't—unless they were inside my head and my body. I hope what I've written on these pages up until this point has given you a little insight. I'm "normal" and not normal at the same time, but isn't everyone? Maybe this will answer the rest!

A Day in My Life

When I am home in LA, I wake up around 6:00 or 7:00 a.m. I go into the kitchen and get my hot green tea ready to go with my grapefruit and apple sprinkled with cinnamon. Then I go into my room, open my Bible, and start reading. I ask God to lead me to a verse I should share with others. I started texting out daily Bible verses a while back but can't remember how or why I started doing it. I find it amazing and humbling how God will guide me to send the exact verse that people need that day. Someone will always text me back, "Thank you! This is *exactly* what I needed to hear right now!" I always reply, "Don't thank me, thank God."

After my daily devotions, I make breakfast, which is typically eggs or egg whites and sautéed veggies, garlic, spices, and avocado. Then I get into my gym clothes and drive over to the gym, my second home. I love being there, and I find it such a motivating environment. We typically do group workouts, usually about four of us in a group. And Eric is not the typical boot-camp, scream-in-your-face kind of trainer. He looks like Thor but acts like a teddy bear. He counts politely as he claps his hands together to keep the beat of our exercises.

After the gym, I come back home, shower, eat a snack, cook lunch so I have that ready, then usually run errands. Depending on how crazy my travel has been, I might squeeze in a thirty-minute power nap. If I have a shoot, appearance, or performance to prepare my body for, I might do two workouts a day, my second around 1:00 or 2:00 p.m. I eat small amounts every two to three hours and keep a strict food curfew: no eating after 7:00 p.m. I stay insanely hydrated and drink green tea twice a day and caffeine-free mint or ginger tea in the evening.

If I have free time, I spend a lot of it at my favorite local café. In fact, I've written a majority of this book at my little spot. It's a French-style place with a little gift shop attached, and it has a homey feel with outdoor seating, big umbrellas, and a peaceful fountain. You'll always find me sitting outside, unless it's one hundred degrees. The café serves organic teas and vegan desserts, and the staff knows me and my order: "Jasmine green tea, as usual?"

My other guilty pleasure is going to the movies with Grant. If a superhero or action move is playing, we're there. I'm such a bro when it comes to movies. My absolute favorite is *The Punisher*, with Thomas Jane. It's based on a Marvel Comics fictional antihero/vigilante.

In the evenings, I cook dinner and eat between 6:00 and 6:30 p.m., always having a tea to finish off my night. I typically cook the same things multiple times a day: eggs and sautéed veggies. I also buy sprouted-grain wraps and tear them into little triangles, put them on a baking sheet, spray them with a little

EVOO, and sprinkle on some onion or garlic salt. Then I pop them in the oven for ten minutes—and *voilà*! Perfect, healthy "chips" that are free of flour, yeast, and corn! I like having two or three of those with every meal. I try to make my last meal of the day my smallest meal. You know the saying, "Breakfast like a prince, lunch like a pauper, and dinner like a peasant." Eric, of course, taught me that! I eat extraordinarily healthy, but I do have one weakness: I love to munch on some sweet potato fries!

I like to wind down by catching up on TV shows from the week that I've missed on Hulu. I love *Once Upon a Time*, *Scandal*, *How to Get Away with Murder*, *The Middle*, and *Criminal Minds*. Thanks to my wild life, I just got to be a guest on the set of *Criminal Minds* and meet the awesome cast and crew. I was welcomed with massive open arms and lots of love. Joe Mantegna is even a fan of *mine*. That is nuts! I try to limit the number of new shows I watch because I'm just too busy to keep up with all of them! I finally caved a few months ago and watched *Game of Thrones*. Now I'm hooked. I binge-watched four entire seasons in a month!

I try to go to bed between 10:00 and 10:30 p.m. Eric also taught me that when it comes to resting your body, the hours before midnight are worth double the ones after! Going to bed early (before midnight) and getting seven to eight consecutive, uninterrupted hours of sleep is extremely important.

I try to pull away from the computer and my phone for at least thirty minutes (on good days an hour) before bed so my brain can get out of work mode and relax. Reading makes me fall asleep fast. My former roommate, Cody, called me a "little Romanian vampire" because I sleep on my back (I trained myself to), don't move a muscle, and breathe so softly it looks like I'm not breathing at all! I have two fans on at night. I like it cold, dark, and quiet, and the sound of the fans lulls me to sleep.

How Do You Walk?

The thing people most want to know about me is how I walk. Well, I put my hands on the ground in front of me, pick up my body a bit, and pull it forward. The skin on my palms is callused and a bit thicker, like you might find on the ball of your foot. I have always had bigger, stronger hands than most girls and have always been self-conscious of them. I assumed they were like this because I used them so much, but it turns out their size is actually in my DNA: my biological mom has "man hands" too! Using my hands to walk definitely requires a lot of upper-body strength. I even underestimated how much work it was in high school, going up and down the stairs multiple times a day all day long, picking up my whole body and propelling it up each step. The school was built in 1912 and had four floors and no elevator! I gained weight when I got out of high school, and I'm convinced it was because I wasn't constantly going up and down stairs with my arms and getting that great workout!

Walking on my hands rarely hurts, even on rough pavement or gravel. I know how not to put as much pressure on my hands on these surfaces. When I was about nine, I did put my hand on a bee (ouch!) in our yard, and that made me a little paranoid. It hurt so badly, and I screamed and cried. I was always looking out for bees—and dog poo—in the grass. Anytime anyone broke glass in our house, my parents were on their hands and knees inspecting the floor like crazy. But for the record: I never cut my hands on anything my brothers managed to knock over. I was always pretty mindful of where I "stepped."

I look like anyone else from the waist up. I've been told I look pretty darn good in a bikini, thank you very much!

My body is in the right proportion; it just looks as if it stops where my upper thighs are.

Deep Thoughts, Deep Feelings

I'm a big thinker. I analyze stuff all the time. *Why did he say that? Why did she do that? Why is there always a traffic jam in LA? What did God intend for me to learn when He delayed my flight three hours? What is the meaning of life?* Okay, perhaps I overanalyze.

I'm always searching for the bigger picture or the reason behind something unexpected. I like to study people and figure out what makes them tick. A lot of life is connecting the dots so you can follow your path where it's supposed to take you. It's important to take a step back and assess things: Where have you been, where are you now, where are you going?

I get lost in the pages of a great book—the Bible being the greatest—and swept away by my vivid imagination. I'm sentimental. I hang on to things forever. I still wear the opal ring Grant gave me for my twenty-first birthday when we lived in Orlando. I have boxes and boxes of photographs, and I am always taking more and studying them with a highly critical eye. For example, I love looking at the hands of Camelia, my birth mom, in pictures. They're the same as mine—strong yet soft.

Laugh It Off

I'm funny. No, really, I've got a wicked sense of humor. If Jimmy (Kimmel or Fallon) had me on, I'd be their favorite guest ever. I crack myself up, which I consider a great gift. It's hard to stay mad at someone when you're laughing—after all, laughter is the best medicine. I look for the humor in almost every situation—even the ones that genuinely stink. I think if you can laugh at yourself, your shortcomings (pun intended), and your mistakes, then you can overcome anything.

Details, Details

When I get stressed, I want to organize things into nice, neat little packages. You could say I'm borderline obsessive-compulsive with all my attention to detail. I used to freak if my DVDs weren't perfectly lined up, if one was pushed out farther than the others. I've eased up a bit, but I do like order. Give me a list, set me a deadline, tell me whatever needs to be done and I'll do it. Just don't leave me hanging! My mind will ricochet off into a million different directions, and that allows the anxiety to build. I'd rather know the reality of the situation—even if it will cause me stress—than have someone sugarcoat it. I'd rather be in on the problem and working toward a solution than be a helpless bystander. Good things come in small packages, people. I'm a grown-up. I'm probably more grown-up than most twentysomethings because I'm an "old soul." I've also been all over the world and experienced things most people never get to in a lifetime.

Super Jen!

I'm a not-so-normal "normal" person. I am not a superhero with superhuman strength (physically or mentally). If some-one's going to be impressed by me, I'd rather it be because

I've done something impressive, not just because I am happy and in shape. Guys— particularly buff, biceps-rippling types of guys—tend to approach me in crowded places and tell me I inspire them. Let me say that again: *I* inspire *them*? What a humbling and interesting experience to have men open up to me in that way. I think it's amazingly beautiful!

Yes, I can climb a flight of stairs with my hands and not break a sweat. Yes, I can haul my own wheelchair into the trunk of a car—and the thing weighs a ton. But let's get real: I'm not Super Jen (though it does have a nice ring to it, doesn't it?).

Lay Off the Lead Hand!

I drive. I was the oldest girl in my grade, so I was first to get my license when I turned sixteen. My car was a red two-door Pontiac Grand Am. One day, on a whim, I asked my parents if we could go to a car lot just to browse, and we ended up getting the Grand Am the very next day—for a great deal! Rigging it for me to drive with no legs was no biggie: a handle was placed to the left of the steering wheel, right under the turn signals, to control the brake and the gas pedals. If anyone else were to drive it, they could just use the pedals like normal. I push down on the handle for gas and forward toward the dash for the brake. My mom always joked I had a "lead hand," because I was always speeding. (For the record, I still drive that car, but I need a new one!)

The night of my sixteenth birthday, the day I got my license, I was backing out of our driveway (it's a tricky driveway, and you have to turn sharply to avoid a ditch) when I rammed right into my brother's truck parked beside me. In my defense, it was nighttime, and the truck was a dark color, but I wound up making a big dent in the side of my new car. Basically, it was a dent and run: I continued driving and met my friend in town. I was horrified and so upset, not to mention afraid my brother and my parents would kill me. When I got home, I worked up the courage to tell them, and they weren't angry at all (in fact, they tried not to laugh, but I caught them).

Parking Pains

These days my wheelchair can make driving a real pain in the butt because I have to fold the chair, then put it in the car. Next, I have to make sure when I park that there's enough space to get the door open and drag it out. Finding a wide enough parking space in SoCal is a feat in and of itself (maybe I am Super Jen and don't know it?).

I rarely ever park in handicapped spots, because I feel other people need them more than I do. But when I do, I sometimes encounter difficult people. One day I was searching for parking at a store in Orlando but there were no spots, so I pulled out my handicapped sign and hung it on my mirror. I was pulling into a handicapped spot when an elderly woman started beating her fists on the passenger-side window. Grant was sitting there and jumped a mile.

"You took that parking spot from my husband," she bellowed, "and you're not handicapped! How dare you!"

First, I was shocked that someone would behave this way. Then I was steaming mad! I pointed to the handicapped sign hanging from my rearview mirror, but she was ranting and raving so much, she didn't notice. So I took it off, slammed it against the windshield, and yelled, "Here! I have a sign, lady!"

That convinced her and she left, but Grant and I just sat there in silence, trying to figure out what the heck had just happened. Then we started laughing! "Oh my gosh, Jen, you *have* to get out," Grant insisted. "She's going to feel like such an idiot when she sees you. Rub it in her face!"

But there was no way I was going to do that. I had absolutely nothing to prove to her. I had a similar incident happen recently here in LA. The parking lots are small, and finding a parking spot is always a game of chance, so I pulled into a handicapped spot to run into a store and get some groceries. As I was pulling out, a lady beside me in a black SUV shouted right in my face through the open window, "Oh yeah, like *you're* handicapped!" This time I didn't blow my top. I just said, in a very calm tone, "Lady, not today . . . you don't want to go there. I actually *do* have a wheelchair." And I pulled away. I was kind of chuckling, and then I thought maybe I should have thanked her. She was at least policing handicapped spots for people who need them. But I guess because I'm young and don't look handicapped when I'm driving, I elicit this frequent reaction from people. You can understand my hesitation to park in a handicapped spot unless I absolutely, positively need to. It's not worth the aggravation!

Ground Level

For someone who spends most of her time in the air as an acrobat, I know this sounds a little strange, but I like being on the floor. When I was in Japan, I was psyched to learn that Japanese people sit on the floor on big pillows and even eat while sitting on the ground.

A Time to Weep

I don't cry often, but as I get older, I'm softening up. One time I was at a karate black-belt graduation (random, I know!) and an elderly man came up to me. He collapsed in my arms and started sobbing. All I could ascertain was that he was a Holocaust survivor. I was so moved, so overwhelmed by his outpouring of emotion that I started to bawl as well and couldn't stop! For this reason, I steer clear of sappy movies. If I know someone dies in a movie, I will not go see it. I got dragged to see *The Fault in Our Stars*, and I swear it scarred me for life.

Milo and Me

I'm a total dog person. Growing up, I had a couple of different dogs: Buddy the cocker spaniel; Eddie the Pomeranian; Speckles the terrier mix; then came my baby. When I was thirteen, I saved up all my money ($150) and bought a crazy little Chihuahua named Milo. I spoiled that dog rotten and treated him like he was my baby. He had so much sass and personality, and he truly thought he was human, not canine. My dad was convinced he could understand English. He would say "We're going to leave" in ten different ways, and Milo would bound toward the door. It became a game. He'd say, "I think we're not going to be in the house anymore" or "Let's be on our way," and Milo would still get it. He loved car rides but hated baths. I'd have to hold him in a towel for twenty minutes after one, and he would cry like a baby in my arms.

Things I Hate, Things I Love

I hate when people are late—it's the fastest way to tick me off!

I hate loud noises, car alarms, and fluorescent lighting. They all put me in a bad mood. I think olives and pickles are gross and kind of weird, and I prefer a good game of tic-tac-toe to chess.

If I had a million dollars, I would hire a very good financial adviser to show me how to make that money work for me. I'd give a bunch of it to my family and to orphanages and adoption centers. And of course, I'd put some away to travel to every country I've ever dreamed of seeing. First class!

I've always seen shooting stars in the sky since I was a kid, when no one else would see them. I thought it was God giving me a wink or a little "God treat." I hadn't seen one in a long time because here in LA, the sky is not that clear (we call it smog). I'd almost forgotten about my shooting stars, and then, out of the blue, one night I caught sight of one. I keep track of these sightings in my journal as a reminder. I could easily forget over and over how many of my prayers have been answered. But God reminds me of His goodness and His miracles whenever I least expect it.

I'm a "small things" kind of girl. I'm easily enamored with and excited by tiny creatures and objects—anything tinier than I am. When I see a little animal, especially a cute little dog, I turn into an overly excited, baby-talking nutcase! I also love dollhouse miniatures, little tea sandwiches, itty-bitty anything. You will never hear me say, "Supersize it."

I'm a sucker for a health food store, where I will comb the aisles in search of chemical-free, "clean" beauty products and pure dark chocolate without any dairy or refined sugar.

I hate loud music, and I'm not much for going to clubs. Give me an acoustic guitar around a campfire or a song in the shower. I'm into jazz, blues, country, and Nashville nights. I'm a girly girl who has bro-ish tendencies. Most days you'll find me in stylish, fitted, bright-colored gym clothes, no makeup, my hair in a ponytail. But I also spend money on manicures and clothes. I love fashion, but I prefer a bargain to spending a ton just for a label.

Regular shirts fit me perfectly—no alterations needed. Same goes for jean shorts, regular shorts, bikini bottoms. Obviously, most of my dresses need to be altered, and my friend Mary Jane, whom I met in the wardrobe department on Britney's tour, lives fifteen minutes from me. She's been a beautiful person in my life. The only pants I ever buy are slightly longer workout shorts/tights. I have them cut and sewn to make the perfect workout wear for me. My mom is really good at sewing, and maybe one day I'll actually learn to do it myself. But for now, I can barely sew on a button!

I love fairy tales, The Hobbit movies, The Hunger Games, and Harry Potter. I've never seen *any* Star Wars movies and have no desire to. I love Julie Andrews and everything she's ever been in. I could watch *Independence Day* with Will Smith over and over and over, and it never gets old! Tyler Perry cracks me up, and one of my favorite restaurants in LA is called The Stinking Rose. They put garlic on everything.

Fall is my favorite season for so many reasons: the changing leaves, the colors, the brisk air, wearing cozy jackets and scarves to ward off the chill. I love sunshine but not the rain.

It brings me down, and for that reason I'm sure I could never live in Seattle! I love hotel robes—the big fluffy ones you wish you could take home in your suitcase but someone would surely notice they were missing—and riding on my brothers' Harleys.

I don't have fears because I don't allow myself to go there. If you focus on a fear, it can become a reality. I only speak positivity and truths from God and His promises. As my faith has increased, my fears have diminished.

I'm very hard to offend. Unless you're straight up being rude (which rarely happens), trust me, I won't take offense if you ask me something or are curious about me. I never want people to feel like they have to walk on eggshells around me.

Marriage and Family

I want to get married and be a mom one day. I want to bring a child (actually, two is a nice number) into this world since it's one of God's greatest miracles. I also want to adopt a child (maybe from Romania) since it was an incredible gift my parents gave to me, and if I adopted a child of my own, the experience would come full circle.

My sister Christina's recent baby shower definitely stirred up some of my emotions regarding marriage and motherhood. It was a special day, and I loved seeing her so grownup: married, a house, dogs, and now having her first baby. It was the first big family event I have attended with both my sisters and Camelia. I met my biological aunt Nina and cousin Carmen for the first time, and they were so welcoming. "You're family," Carmen—who was also pregnant—told me. We played a silly shower game called "Guess the Size of

Mommy's Tummy!" and had to hold up a measuring tape to Christina's waist with our guestimate. Well, I overmeasured big-time—I pretty much insinuated she was the size of a house. Everyone was dying of laughter, and Christina was so happy. Just then a thought entered my head: *This is pretty nice. This could be me.* It didn't feel so strange or foreign.

I have never been in a rush to have kids, and I've told myself I'll wait until I'm totally ready. But maybe I finally am? In the past, I didn't want to feel tied down to anyone or any one place. I love to feel "free." But after seeing how happy Christina was, something just clicked for me.

My plan is to have as much of a clean slate as possible before I settle down. I've said I want to be debt-free and relieved of any emotional baggage from my past relationships before I get married. I can happily say that I'm now debt-free and have done some major work in the baggage department! Praise God! I've started praying for God to put the pieces back in my heart that I gave away to past boyfriends. I know marriage is one of the biggest decisions I'll ever make, and I believe in preparing for it. Think about it: you prepare for most big things in your life—like college—for years. Olympians train their whole lives! I've given marriage a lot of careful thought and consideration (I told you, I like to overanalyze). I believe marriage starts with two people who are in total alignment with God, themselves, their faith, their confidence in who they are and where they're going. I can actually picture my future wedding ceremony (though the groom is still fuzzy). I've never wanted a big wedding, just a tiny ceremony outside, surrounded by only the closest people in my life. Simple, that's how I want it. Honestly, I'd have no problem eloping, except that I think my mom would really like to see her only daughter get married! I've never understood spending thousands of dollars on a dress, flowers, and reception—a wedding that lasts just a few short hours. My honeymoon, however, will be extravagant! I've always dreamed of going to Tahiti for two weeks and staying in one of those bungalows in the middle of the water with the glass floor, getting massages on the beach . . .

Making Connections

Did I mention I'm also a big daydreamer? I see things— beautiful, amazing, breathtaking things—that I want to do and be in my life. If you had asked me when I was a little girl what I wanted to be when I grew up, I never would have been able to picture my life now. Yes, I'm a performer, but performing is a way for me to connect with people. So perhaps I'm a "connector"? Is that even a profession? But that's how I see myself, and frankly, if it's not already a job, someone should consider putting it on LinkedIn. Why not be a force for uniting people? Someone who brings others closer to their dreams and closer to God. I want to do something important with my life, something meaningful. I want to do things that matter. I see this book as my first step in that direction. I want to take it on the road and meet with and speak to as many people as I can. I want to share my life and my love for God.

On the Road Again

I have a really good long-term memory—long and detailed. I simply can hit the replay button in my mind, and memories come back to me, clear as day—faces, places, and entire conversations. Because I travel so often, I've met many fascinating people on planes and in airports. In 2015, the longest stretch of time I was home was four consecutive weeks. I seem to always have a half-packed suitcase open on my bedroom floor. It's just easier. I hate to pack and unpack, and this way I'm less likely to forget something.

One time, on a layover in Las Vegas, I saw rapper LL Cool J at my gate. We were on the same flight, and everyone was running up and taking pictures with him, but I never want to be *that* person, so I hung back and waited until the mob dissipated. Finally, I grabbed a quick pic and gushed, "You're awesome!" before going back to my seat. About five minutes later, someone from his entourage came over to me.

"LL would like to talk with you," she said.

I looked around. "Me? You're talking to me?"

She nodded and escorted me over to his group of seven people.

I was speechless—and I don't get speechless. I just stood there, staring and starstruck.

"I just think you're beautiful and amazing," he said. "I'm fascinated by you. Tell me your story!"

So I did. I told him all about myself, and his entourage gathered around me in a semicircle, hanging on every word.

I've had numerous other star encounters. I'm a huge fan of the TV show *Supernatural*, and one day at LAX, I saw the actor Jared Padalecki, who plays Sam on the series. I was a huge fan but didn't want to bother him. So I asked the flight attendant if she would mind telling him I would like to meet him. A few moments later, he came back not just to say hi but to sit and chat with me! We talked for a half hour! Another time, Dwayne "The Rock" Johnson came into my gym to work out. I didn't want him to think I was a crazy fan, and now I'm kind of kicking myself. Maybe someday . . .

God has given me so many opportunities that when I start to list them, I'm humbled, grateful, and frankly, a little overwhelmed. Not too long ago I performed in Tokyo in front of a TV audience of seventeen million! I loved Japan. The people are generally shorter than here in the United States, so everything is lower: sinks, towel racks, tables. Just perfectly Jen-sized! I also noticed that people didn't stare at me—maybe because they're all so polite! I was there for two weeks and tried all kinds of interesting foods, including squid intestines, cow tongue, and every type of sashimi imaginable, which was so fresh it tasted like it had just been swimming in the sea. I'm a pretty adventurous eater. I'll try just about anything once. I've had camel burgers in Dubai and kangaroo skewers in Australia, where I also learned how to surf. I went quad biking in the middle of the Arabian desert, swam with a dolphin in Hawaii, zip-lined through the Costa Rican rain forest, and got certified in scuba diving in Dubai. I've also spent time in Thailand and Singapore, and kayaked with monkeys on the island of Ko Lanta.

In every city, state, and country I visit, God always puts beautiful people in my life whom I call my angels. These folks are armed with humble hearts and truly radiate God's love. At least one person everywhere I have traveled has loved on me, taken me out to dinner, bought me groceries, cooked for me, given me gifts, provided me a palatial studio to stay in with my own private beach access, taken me for a massage or to get my nails done, chauffeured me around sightseeing, and on and on! Just recently a very kind hotel owner provided me with a place to stay in Thailand that had air-conditioning, a flushing toilet, and a hot shower—all very sought-after commodities in Thailand—and I didn't have to sleep with a mosquito net! I never have to worry about my safety (God always has me protected) or having the proper resources or a place to stay. God always has my back and puts these precious people in my life. I pray for the people who bless me—I hope they are doubly blessed for their generosity. You all know who you are, and please realize I am beyond grateful.

Every so often I have to pinch myself. God has blessed me so much. He put all of these wonderful opportunities before me, and the only payment He wants is for me to love Him. The other thing I frequently think about is that I'm not even thirty yet. Will I ever run out of exciting adventures? Have I maxed out my quota for cool life experiences? I doubt it. I think the world is a wide, wonderful place meant to be explored from top to bottom, coast to coast, continent to continent. With every new place I visit, with every new person I meet, I'm continually growing and rethinking who I am and who I want to be. I soak it all in.

So if you check back with me a year or two from now . . . who knows? I might be taking home the coveted mirror ball trophy on *Dancing with the Stars* or rocketing through outer space. As far as I'm concerned, neither is out of the realm of possibility.

Medals of Honor

I've been particularly humbled by all the awards I've received over the years. Dominique and I gave a TEDx speech in Akron, Ohio, which was pretty awesome. I was deeply honored to receive the Muscle Beach Courage Award from Joe

Wheatley, who runs Muscle Beach/Venice, and I received the Inspiration Award from Shane's Inspiration, a beautiful company that builds all-inclusive playgrounds around the world. I was an honored guest speaker for the Special Olympics here in SoCal and received a Disability in Sports Award from the Disability Rights Legal Center in Los Angeles.

I received one of the coolest awards of my career from the Zayed Higher Organization for Humanitarian Care & Special Needs after speaking in Abu Dhabi. The words on the plaque are written in Arabic, and I don't even have to know what they say to feel proud.

I would say my ultimate accolade came in 2015 when I was honored as a "legend" and received an award from the World Acrobatics Society. I was shocked. *Me? A legend? Am I even old enough?* As I received my award, I was surrounded by Olympians and VIPs/performers/artists in the circus community. Most everyone there was fifteen to thirty years older than I was. My sister's entire '96 Olympic team was recognized in the category as well, so she and I got to see each other receive our honors. It was such a special evening.

Here's the thing: Do I need medals or trophies or plaques or titles to make me feel good about myself? No. For me, it's not about the recognition or affirmation. Instead, I look at each of these awards as motivation to keep doing what I'm doing, to keep dreaming bigger. It's not about the prize; it's about celebrating the journey. I'm incredibly proud of and grateful for how far I've come and how far I still want to go.

Jen Bricker is an author, aerialist, and motivational speaker. A state champion in power tumbling, she has traveled internationally with Britney Spears's Circus Tour and has appeared as a headliner at the prestigious Palazzo Hotel in Las Vegas, New York's Lincoln Center, the Shangri-La Hotel in Dubai, and the Nippon Budokan in Tokyo. She has been featured on numerous news shows, including HBO's *Real Sports*, ABC's *20/20*, EPSPN's *Versus*, and *Good Morning America*. She is currently living in Los Angeles and has added a successful speaking career to her list of accomplishments, including a TEDx talk and several other speeches around the world, from Abu Dhabi and Hong Kong to Malaysia and Thailand. Through her faith, drive, and determination, she continues to prove to herself and others that everything is possible.

CONNECT
WITH

JENBRICKER.COM

f   JEN BRICKER

📷 @JENBRICKER

🐦 @JENBRICKER1

LIKE THIS BOOK?

Consider sharing it with others!

- Share or mention the book on your social media platforms. Use the hashtag **#EverythingIsPossible**.

- Write a book review on your blog or on a retailer site.

- Pick up a copy for friends, family, or strangers! Anyone who you think would enjoy and be challenged by its message.

- Share this message on Twitter or Facebook: **"I loved #EverythingIsPossible by @JenBricker//@ReadBakerBooks"**

- Recommend this book for your church, workplace, book club, or class.

- Follow Baker Books on social media and tell us what you like.

 Facebook.com/ReadBakerBooks

 @ReadBakerBooks